PARIS MATCH

AGATHA GOES to FRANCE

Siân Pattenden

✱ SHORT BOOKS

First published in 2008 by

Short Books

3A Exmouth House

Pine Street

London EC1R 0JH

10 9 8 7 6 5 4 3 2 1

Copyright ©

Siân Pattenden 2008

A CIP catalogue record for this book
is available from the British Library.

ISBN 978–1-906021-30-6

CONTENTS

1. PACKED OFF TO FRANCE

A gatha held her cardigan up to the light so she could examine it closely. There were moist brown lumps all over the garment, which smelt of a non-specific meat. She took her jeans out of the washing machine and found that they too were covered in this lumpy stuff. It did not take her long to realise that all her clothes had been ruined. And then she spotted the open can of dog food on the machine. Demone – her French exchange and her supposed friend – had played yet another trick on her. How dare she?

Demone Canard was, perhaps, the worst girl Agatha Bilke had ever met. And, considering how horrible Agatha had been in the past, this was truly incredible.

At first, Agatha had been excited at the prospect of going to stay with a family in France. She had seen a TV

programme about Calais, the
famous seaside town which
people visited to buy lager. And
she had been intrigued by the
thought that this country,
divided from Great Britain by
merely a few miles of sea, was
so different. The people
appeared cultured, sophisticated

and yet charming. The kids looked cool – they all wore
leather jackets. It certainly seemed a better place than
Rottington Town...

Agatha's school had started teaching French and she
liked the way the words lilted and tilted, ebbed and flowed.
Her favourite phrases so far were: "*merveilleux*" (marvel-
lous); "*vous êtes un espèce d'idiot*" (you are an idiot) and
"*déblaye le terrain, gendarme!*" (push off, policeman!). She had
started to fall for the whole French thing: from now on, she
told her mother, she would only eat baguettes; she took to
wearing a stripy Breton jumper and put a poster of the
09.15 ferry to Dieppe on her wall.

The idea of finding a French exchange had come from
Agatha's elder sister Margaret. About six months before
this washing machine disaster, Margaret had swanned off to

France, announcing she was going to become a property developer. A fan of the hare-brained scheme, Margaret had "faaaaallen in love" with an ornate mansion called the Villa de Mer whilst on a weekend break. A little tatty and located on a main road, it was going at an attractive price. If she rented it out, she would make a fortune. Margaret knew she had the potential to make property her livelihood; her ambition was to have a "portfolio", whatever that was.

For the first few months, Margaret stayed in an apartment nearby, just to make sure things went smoothly. And it was at about that time that Agatha started to express an interest in all things Gallic. "Why doesn't little sis come out to the South of France?" suggested Margaret. She would put an ad in the local *supermarché* for a French exchange over the summer. This way Bilke junior would have a ~~much-deserved~~ holiday in the sun, learn more of the language and broaden her horizons – *and* Margaret could keep an eye on her.

A family was soon found and a date was set for Agatha to go and stay with them. The daughter, Demone, was willing to share her day-to-day life with the English girl. Agatha was delighted. The dream would soon become a reality. She would be setting sail, across the seas, to the land of opportunity (or was that America?). She would see those cool kids in leather jackets! She would eat a lot of garlic! She might even behave herself for once.

The Canard family, too, seemed thrilled — perhaps their young guest would bring with her that curious delicacy, Marmite? Or she might sleep with a bowler hat next to her bed. Of course, they had not been told of Agatha's history. If they had been even half aware of the list of crimes she had perpetrated — arson, trespass, kidnap, theft, medical malpractice, carjacking, drugging a minor etc. — they would surely not have wanted this visitor residing with them at all.

2. LOG ON, LOG OFF

Was it all inevitable? How did Anglo-French relations disintegrate so quickly?

After a week, Demone and Agatha were barely on speaking terms. The French girl had taken an instant dislike to Bilke — maybe because she was not interested in computers. For Demone was obsessed by the internet — real life did not interest her one bit. She had ignored Agatha at first, and then become spiteful. On Monday, chilli powder had found its way into *all* Agatha's meals (including breakfast). On Tuesday, Agatha noticed that the pages of her *Compliment Bonjour!* French phrasebook

Instead of a cheery "hello" in the morning, Demone would cry "log on!" and run to the screen

had been glued together. On Wednesday, her hairbrush had been dipped in mustard. Meanwhile, Demone just sat in her bedroom all day, squinting at her PC.

She was tiny; she looked like a doll. Her hair was cut in a severe black bob and she had bandy legs with four moles on her left knee. She couldn't have looked less brittle had she been made out of breadsticks.

On occasion, she would address Agatha in English, but this was just to mutter how much she thought her French exchange was "the simple" and "not a vestibule who is a computer literate". Mostly, she talked digi-chat.

Instead of a cheery "hello" in the morning, she would cry "log on!" and run to the screen. If she was irritated she would command "reload!" If she hated something she would shout "spam!" – the opposite of that was "anti-spam!" She had hijacked a language which was already an amalgam of English, code, techno-jargon and American slang – and tailored it to her own needs. Most of the time, she sounded like a robot.

What made it more irritating was that the Canard parents were never around to notice what was happening. Demone's father was a factory worker: gruff and hairy. The mum made soap in the bathtub and flogged it to the local markets (and online to English people who thought it was made by romantic peasants who worked the hillsides). Their only child was precious to them; although they sometimes forgot her name.

Brioche was a grim industrial town and the Canards' home was near a glue factory, a polyester factory, a stationery warehouse and two large blocks of flats. Needless to say, the living arrangements left a lot to be desired. The food provision, for instance, was lacking. The only fresh fruit specimen was a lonely orange in a bowl, and that looked as if it were a few weeks old. From the day she arrived, Agatha found herself permanently hungry – she was fed on a diet of oatmeal, a rubbery sort of cheese and, for pudding, strawberry jelly which had unidentified bits in it. There was always a strong smell of coffee on the hob and jars of rough pâté which, left out for days, attracted a larger type of fly than Agatha was used to seeing back home. The sleeping quarters were not pleasant either. Her bed was in the cellar – next to the deep freeze which hummed at night – with a rough blanket which scratched her face.

Life outside the Canard home was hardly better. Demone never seemed to go to school. On the one day she *did* bother to accompany Agatha, she walked several paces in front of her, made her carry all the bags and when they

Brioche was a grim industrial town and the Canards' home
was near a glue factory, a polyester factory, a stationery warehouse
and two large blocks of flats

arrived she made it very clear she didn't want to sit next to her new English chum in class. Instead, Demone plonked herself down next to an ugly boy called Bernard, who wore thick glasses and had the first rumblings of a moustache — although he was only thirteen years old. Demone and Bernard then proceeded to speak in speedy French to each other, never once addressing Bilke.

The other kids seemed wildly cool by comparison. They *did* wear leather jackets and some drove around on mopeds. The girls looked really mature; they wore jewellery and chewed gum. They seemed bored in lessons and talked about "*ennui*". Agatha was amazed: in Rottington the girls wore velour tracksuits and some of them had pierced belly-buttons. The twelve-year-olds looked, at most, fourteen, and acted as if they were eight. But these French girls were everything Agatha had dreamt of! How had she got stuck with Demone?

That afternoon, instead of hanging around on motorbikes after school like everyone else, Demone and Bernard dragged Agatha to the public library, where they sat in front of yet more computer screens and ate a very smelly block of cheese together. Agatha sat in the corner, bored — she

threw chewed-up tissue paper at Demone and looked at the books to see if there were any pictures of naked people in them.

The following day, Agatha was yet again sitting on the edge of Demone's bed watching her surf the net. This was unutterably dull. Demone could not stop looking at the BeBois.com cyber-networking site. She tapped away under various aliases, pretending that she liked jazz music and frequented late-night bars. A pop-up advert sprung from the webpage she was looking at: an awful jingle which was promoting a fizzy drink that seemed to be called *Burp Burp*. It was performed by a pixelated monkey and Demone started singing along. If only her virtual friends knew that the girl who made herself appear to be so worldly on the web was such a geek, thought Agatha.

"Bon bon bon
Achetez le Burp Burp! Bon bon bon
Have you le slurp slurp?"

Then the monkey belched and a cartoon tree fell over. It was the worst song in the world, but Demone was really getting into it. She sang as if her life depended on it; it was a right racket.

slurp! slurp!

Agatha contemplated smashing all of the girl's posses-
sions with a big brick, but knew that she probably wouldn't
be able to get away with that – she felt rather more
vulnerable over here in France, away from Rottington.
And, at this particular moment, she was feeling especially
exposed. After the washing machine "accident", Demone
had given her a pair of corduroy trousers and an itchy
woollen jumper with a ship on it to wear. So now she
looked like a geek too. It was high summer, and the top

was too hot and the trousers too long. (Was this another practical joke?)

Couldn't the girls go into the town and find something else to do? They had already been to the swimming pool, but they hadn't had enough money to get in. They had peeked through the railings and seen the cool kids sitting around, eating ice creams and throwing towels at each other. It looked like fun. Agatha had heard that there was also an ice rink nearby.

"Hey, Demone. Will your mum give us some money tomorrow?" she asked. "Perhaps we could go skating."

Demone squealed "Spam!" then continued to sing the silly fizzy drink song.

"Come on, we have to find something to do…" persisted Agatha. " Is Bernard around?"

Her host still sang the song, louder now, as if to block Agatha out. "*Burp burp / Slurp slurp!*"

"You've been sitting at that frizzing computer all week now and I've had enough," said Agatha. "You're boring, spiteful, mean and conceited! *Tu es un espèce d'idiot!*"

Demone slapped the visitor on the cheek. "Shut down!" she screamed at her.

"You're worse than… I am!" cried Agatha, who started to pinch her opponent's arm.

At which point Canard spat in the English girl's face.

Arghhh! Time to show the French girl what British people were made of – Agatha came from the land of tug o' war, not airy-fairy croquet. She seized the girl's hair and yanked as hard as she could. Then she yanked again, just for good measure. But, for a little 'un, Demone was made of strong stuff. She kicked Agatha in the shins, pulled her nose, tweaked an ear and screamed at such a high pitch that a passing horse on its way to the glue factory began to vibrate.

Agatha yelled, caught Demone's wrist and bit into it. *This is quite good fun*, she thought. It almost made up for not going ice skating.

The fighting was halted by a screech from the computer and flashing lights. Both girls stared at the screen, as a familiar face appeared and neon-coloured green stuff started oozing from her nose. It was a horrible image: truly terrifying to man and beast (and insects and other stuff). The screeching got louder – green stuff was now erupting from the hooter at an alarming rate, like a volcano upside down. Then Agatha realised that this cartoon was a depiction of... herself!

"Demone!" she shouted, stunned. "What's going on? Is that *me*?" She watched in horror as the animation ended with green snot all over the screen and the message: *Agatha Bilke: The Snottiest Girl In The World.*

Of course, this was not true — Agatha's nose was quite presentable — but the screen shot made her look like a fool. Demone had scanned her passport picture into the computer and used the Photosnot programme to do the rest. And she had done this while Agatha had been in the room, while pretending to email her cyber pals.

"It *is* you! Very clever, snot-face!" shouted the computer hacker, with a laugh that sounded like a cheese grater on a very busy, very cheesy day. "And I 'ave put it on your own special Bebois page, hahahahahahahah!"

This was low-down, juvenile and petty. It looked like Agatha had posted the page herself — as if she wanted everyone to know she was proud of producing luminous phlegm. Now, to make matters worse, people were beginning to post their comments below, saying that they knew the girl and, yes, her nose had always dribbled. Many continued to reveal her awful past, albeit with bad spelling and poor grammar:

- August 23 10:40
dreampony99, Rottington/gbr
Agatha woz always vary snotty. She woz naughty

too and once tried to pull all of my hair off.

Comment No. 830122

•   August 23 10:50
TheSpinach, Rottington/gbr
I used to know her when she is young and she is trouble, innit. Fire engines were always coming round her house, knowworrimean? Safe.

Comment No. 830123

•   August 23 12:19
humphreydocs2005, London/gbr
I remember this girl from our famous Clinic. Perhaps we should all give her the benefit of the doubt, even though she is absolutely awful and terrorised her fellow-patients.

Comment No. 830166

[Offensive? Unsuitable? Report this comment.]

"Demone! How could you?" The fact was that the French girl hardly knew Agatha, yet she'd so far done all she could to make her life hell. At least when Bilke didn't like someone, she had *taken time* to note their bad points.

"My pleasure, chum," she said sarcastically.

"How did you get my passport? Give it back!" Agatha held out her hand.

But Demone just pointed out of the bedroom window. All Agatha could see was the polyester factory. Unless it was the stationery warehouse. Or the glue factory.

"The workers over there," she said. "They love your beautiful documentation! Hahahah!"

Demone was cold and calculating; digital and deceiving. She didn't care that Agatha disliked her; she didn't have time for the real world. She was wrapped up in gigabytes and microchips – and she was beginning to believe that she was invincible. She started humming that ridiculous fizzy drink tune as it popped up again.

"You will not win!" Agatha whispered under her breath. "You will suffer the way I have suffered" – and she was deadly serious. As Demone continued to whine the trite melody, her English "chum" suddenly had a great idea.

3. MONKEY MAGIC

In the old days, when fires were fires and Agatha frightened everyone she met, life had been straightforward. She had been bent on destruction and determined to be bad, and destructive and bad she invariably was. However, ever since she had set foot in France, roles seemed to have been reversed.

Agatha had been double-crossed and tripped up at every turn. Demone was always one step ahead and this from someone who seemingly had no reason to be mean. Agatha had not, for example, arrived and put biro marks on the furniture. She had not shoved anyone down a crevice or a ravine – even at Demone's school she had listened to the teacher jabber away in French and not set fire to anyone's rucksack. So why was she the target of Demone's hate? She could not linger, waiting to find out; she needed to retaliate now.

Leaving Demone cackling in her swivel chair, in front of the computer, Agatha ventured out onto the landing and downstairs. Monsieur and Madame Canard were out, as usual. The girl ran down to the cellar and located the chest freezer. This must contain something that she could use for a revenge attack. The light bulb had gone, so she rummaged around, barely able to see what she was doing. There were things with claws, something slimy that smelt like old sports headbands do – and a few boxes at the bottom. She pulled out one of these and saw a picture of a frog, with a big arrow pointing to its legs. Ideal! She carefully crept up to the kitchen, opened the packet and slowly stuffed the frozen limbs, one by one, into the four-slot toaster. *This* should make an impression.

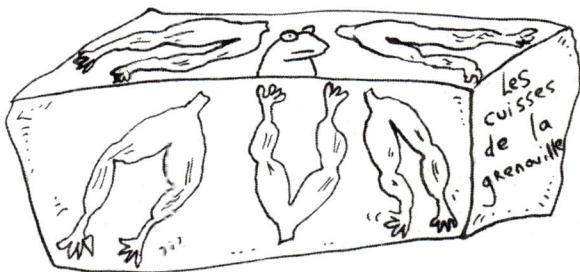

Agatha would now need to find something to document the evidence. Did the Canards have a camcorder? Most families owned one nowadays – they all wanted to film themselves being happy at the seaside, or smiling on a zoo trip. Agatha rifled through the pine cabinet in the living room.

"Agatha! More comments from ze friends on your Bebois page!" Demone was calling her from upstairs. "Hey, where are you? Make me a *cup of tea!*"

Agatha found all sorts in the cabinet: an old tape recorder, a book about the Foreign Legion, a ruler and an ancient ham croissant – but no camcorder. She had to think it through – if they did have one, where would it be kept?

She looked in all the usual places; then some strange ones: the fridge, under the sink, in the oven... She glanced in the knife drawer then went to the washing machine.

Aha! There it was, sitting on the top. Agatha shuddered, a quivery, quavery feeling that made her shoulders feel as if they were made out of meringues – flaky and light. Of course, she had to press "play" – *just in case someone had been secretly filming...*

Crisis! She had been filmed taking her soiled washing out of the machine! Agatha looked for all the world like a lost, lonely little girl. This was too much. She had been angry after the fight with Demone, but now she was raging — raging like a wildebeest trying to find a space in a full car park. The girl not only wanted to make her life impossible, she wanted to remind her time and time again. And it was probably the next thing to be added to her Bebois page.

Agatha pressed "rewind" and found the beginning of the tape. She started recording her own wobbly film. She called up to her so-called friend: "Demone! I have made your tea! Come and get it!"

The French girl wandered downstairs into the kitchen and saw her filming. She looked worried.

"*Spam! Log off! Log off!*"

She grabbed for the camcorder but Agatha moved away and switched the toaster on.

"Give me zat!"

"No, Demone. You filmed me taking my washing out of the machine — it *proves* it was no accident! And so... here is *your* 'accident'..."

As Demone approached, snarling, a plague of one thousand crispy frogs' legs erupted from the toaster. The tiny amphibian limbs filled the air and bounced off the walls like popcorn in a pan. Then the toaster caught fire and Demone started hollering and jumping up and down. Small green sticks were everywhere.

The tiny amphibian limbs filled the air and bounced off the walls like popcorn in a pan

"*Crash! Crash! Force quit!*"

She started to cry.

Agatha pressed "stop" — she had plenty of material. Ripping out the memory card, she threw the camera on the ground. It bounced — and three bits of plastic fell off.

"My camcorder!" Demone was distraught as she picked it up. Agatha did not care. She giggled as she ran out of the house and towards the public library. She logged onto a public computer by copying the card number of the person next to her and uploaded the footage on BeBois.com. It took almost an hour, but when she had finished she was triumphant. Wailing as burnt frogs' legs rained around her, Demone looked like a total prat — and would now be exposed before all her cyber pals. Agatha punched the stale library air with her fist in celebration. She had won!

Suddenly there was a kerfuffle at the door. The gendarmes were running towards her. *Zut!*

A tall man with a bushy moustache and a bulbous nose gripped Agatha tightly by her victory arm. He bellowed at her, as if she was further away than she actually was.

"We 'ave reason to believe," he yelled, through the nose, "zat you are using zis computer wiv ze illegality."

Had the librarian snitched on her? She had seen those elephants TV programmes about people who bring a jar of chutney across the channel and get arrested by customs for introducing diseases to rich people. Did she have any chutney about her person? She didn't think so.

The official took a bit of bright yellow plastic from his pocket and dangled it in front of her.

"We know who you are, Mademoiselle Bilké from ze Rottington, England," he shouted, nose a-bulbin'. "We 'ave been told to keep an eye on you, hence *le tag*. Bilké, you are now marked."

"*Déblaye le terrain, gendarme!*" said Agatha, hopefully.

The phrase had no effect – the policeman clipped the tag around the girl's ankle and pulled it so tight it looked like it would never come off. What was worse, Agatha could hear it vibrating; a small sound which – to Agatha – was like an ant stuck in a plastic beaker.

Everyone in the library was staring. Agatha looked around and saw a shadow lurking in the doorway... Margaret? Her sister?

Urgh. What on earth was she doing here?

Bilke senior was angry. She elongated her "a"s even more than usual.

"The Can*aaaaaaaaaaaaaaaaaaaaa*rd family has phoned me," she said sternly. "You h*aaa*ve been a n*aaaaaaaaaaaaaaaa*ughty girl. They will no longer have you in their house, so you're

Agatha looked around and saw a shadow lurking in the doorway... Margaret? Her sister?

going to have to come with me."

"Look, Margaret, whatever they say, I can explain... I tried to get on with Demone, I am INNOCENT!" pleaded Agatha, as Margaret grasped her wrist and led her out of the library... even though she had just filmed a load of piping-hot frogs falling on a schoolgirl.

Her sister said nothing as she marched her out. However, rather than leaving in an old van or having to walk, they were greeted by a chauffeur who helped them into Margaret's waiting limousine.

If this was a punishment, thought Agatha, then she rather liked it. Had Margaret found success as a property owner?

4. YACHT HOT HOT HOTSPOT

"I'm afraid we are going to my deluxe holiday ap*aaa*rtment in Cannes," said the bigger Bilke. She was dressed head to toe in Flannelle, the most desirable label for a woman with an eye on a good investment. Her nails were manicured and painted with Oriental symbols. Her hair was coiffed. She looked a bit like a newsreader.

"You will live in s*t*ate-of-the-*aaaa*rt splendour overlooking the sea, eating the finest grub known to hum*aaa*nkind — *aaaaaaaaaaaa*nd drinking very strong coffee," she informed her sister. "I will throw in some pickled onion sandwiches too, if you're lucky. Of course, you will need to stop putting *aaa*nimals in toasters."

Agatha told her it was retaliation, for all the horrible things Demone had done to her.

"Well, as I h*aaa*ve seen no evidence… I will take you at your word."

Why had Agatha not been offered this treatment sooner? She had suffered a week of humiliation with the Canards, when all the while Margaret had been sitting – nay, lounging with her mouth slightly open – in the lap of luxury. How on earth had Margaret suddenly got so rich? Agatha had to accept that this was one of those "learning" experiences – and now she had landed on her feet. Why should she worry when she had a rosy future ahead of her? No more cyber bullies. No more snotty noses. No more frogs' legs.

The truth was that Margaret was pleased to have Agatha back in the fold – but not because she had missed her, or anything nice like that. Instead, she thought that her hardnosed little sister might prove herself rather useful. Margaret was learning to become ruthless when it came to money matters – and now Agatha owed her a favour.

The older Bilke's mind was like a very small spaghetti factory. Ideas would form like long strings of fanciful notions, then somehow they would pile up against each other, forming one big lump and eventually a large mass of mush inside her head. To say that her thoughts were stringy and sometimes rather chewy — well, that would be exactly right.

Margaret's bonce was full of troublesome noodles today. The tenants in the Villa de Mer had failed to pay their rent for the last two months and Margaret smelt a rat. ~~She had even smelt a woodlouse~~. She had tried, on various occasions, to go round and evict them, but she had always come up against an obstruction of one sort or another. Legally, it was a minefield — in fact it would have been easier if it was a minefield because then the tenants would have ~~had their feet blown off by now~~ known that it was too dangerous to stay.

The problem was that the residents of the villa were no run-of-the-mill tycoons. They were the one and only Folbecks, proprietors of *Folbeck Mints* — whose cravat-wearing posh-boy son, Holbeck, had become good friends with Agatha at the Rottington hospital last summer. Margaret hoped that her sister would be able to coax the family out by getting round the boy, who would persuade his parents that they must leave. But she wasn't telling Agatha any of that yet.

MARGARET'S MIND
(fuLL of SPAGHETTI)

The Folbecks were, Margaret had noted, stinking rich. When she had shown them around the property they had not made the customary "ooh" and "aah" noises at the stunning proportions, light and space – instead the mother had complained about "attention to detail" and "poor quality fixtures and fittings". Such high-octane moaning was surely a mark of people with more money than sense. But Margaret was starting to hear stories around the town – that the family had been ruined by the recent Exploding Mints Scandal – where packets of their Folbeck Imperials had randomly combusted because they were fitted with illegal tracking devices. Local people claimed that they had not seen the family for days, weeks. They may have once had pots of cash, thought Margaret, but were they *still* loaded? Why had they suddenly stopped paying the rent? And what was all this about teams of children running riot in the place? It was up to Agatha to find out.

☆ ☆ ☆

Margaret told the driver to stop outside a block of art deco apartments and Agatha was awestruck. The lobby was plushly carpeted in red, with pearly white walls and tiny butterflies painted on the ceiling. A wizened old man in a blazer stood by a walnut desk which had further butterfly figures carved into it — and a lizard doing the splits.

Up the lift to the fourth floor, into the flat and Agatha almost fainted. They could see across the Mediterranean — the apartment overlooked yachts, film stars, bigger yachts and more successful film stars. The interior of the flat was white, with huge Corinthian pillars everywhere, a gold tiger statuette in the corner and niches in the walls where busts of great composers were placed. It was not only sumptuous, it was *cultured*. There was a cabinet full of Favergé eggs — from the historic display cabinets of the Russian monarchy — terribly expensive but not actually edible (the eggs, not the monarchy — although they weren't very nice to chew either). In the bathroom, a marble turtle was placed on the free-standing bath, and out of its mouth frothed gallons of bubbly water — even when the taps were turned off. Its feet held soaps and fine tapestries.

"I do so love the *nouveau riche* style," said Margaret proudly, as she

went to the tiny fridge and poured herself a *jus de can-teloupe*.

"Would you like a *jus d'éléphante*? So refreshing. The life out here, I must say, is a cut *aaaaaaaaaaa*bove."

Agatha had never seen her sister in such an opulent setting before. What a good idea this property lark was. Making deals, borrowing money, buying turtles. This was something Agatha herself should consider going into. She would obviously have to go to school first – one that she hadn't been excluded from – and take Business Studies and wear a suit and try not to look bored. But it could be a great life, a *good* life. Helping people live in nice houses was certainly a very decent thing to do. It really did add something to the "collective good".

☆ ☆ ☆

Margaret shoved a pickled onion into her juice and slobbered a bit, as if the spaghetti in her mind was unravelling – and dangling down the back of her throat. She turned around and smiled at her young sister broadly.

Of course, this was all an act – the flat, the juice, the eggs – and she hoped that Agatha was falling for it. What she kept telling herself *not* to reveal – although she soon would

In the bathroom, a marble turtle was placed by the free-standing bath, and out of its mouth frothed gallons of bubbly water – even when the taps were turned off

— was that she was near breaking point financially. All this opulence was a front — put on for the benefit of her virtually non-existent clients. The eggs were on loan and she was desperate to get the Folbecks out — she would be declared bankrupt if she didn't evict them in the next 24 hours. It was easy for a business empire to go down, you know. The would-be property tycoon had learnt all about it from *Claire Tomato's Property Hot Hot Hotspot!* on TV.

Margaret had been visiting the Villa de Mer every day for three weeks now. Once or twice she had come up against Holbeck — who had been wearing a strange floppy wig — but most of the time no one answered the door, no matter how long she waited. She heard children's laughter and tried to look round the back, but all to no avail. Someone had added extra locks to the gates so she was denied way of entry. When Margaret got the call from Demone's parents, so upset that this Agatha had "ruined our baby's life!", it suddenly occured to her that she could turn things to her advantage. In Margaret's flawed logic, i.e. in her spaghetti brains, Agatha was the perfect person to get the Folbecks out. Perhaps if Holbeck saw her at the door he would be eager to catch up for old times' sake and invite her in. He would really listen to Ag — seeing as they'd been such great chums. Margaret was certain that her plan would work. But if Agatha *knew* Holbeck was in there before she went round, she would not want to go through with the mission.

☆ ☆ ☆

Margaret had felt manipulated by Agatha ever since she had first thrown her toys out of the pram all those years ago. She may have been a decade Agatha's senior, but she increasingly needed to feel superior to her sister – and here was her chance. If she managed not to reveal her troubles, and Agatha successfully got the Villa de Mer back for her, then no one need be the wiser. For a few magnificent days she would keep up the façade – that of the loaded businesswoman – until the performance became reality. Margaret glanced in the mirror, smoothed her eyebrows with her middle finger and raised her chin. She would not be intimidated as she had been before. This time, Agatha would do exactly what she was told.

The only dent in Margaret's already-quite-dented plan was the yellow tag, which was micro-chipped to ring an alarm back at the police station if Agatha was out after a 7pm curfew. Would the police rush to find her on her first offence? Margaret wondered. She had to take that risk. And anyway, what could they do to Agatha, other than just take her back to her sister's? She doubted they would even notice.

Agatha, meanwhile, was still wandering through the apartment amazed, blissfully unaware of Margaret's troubles. She was more interested in the fact she would never have to work at any ~~boring~~ proper job – ever. And she would never see that toasted frog Demone again. Everything had turned out perfect after all.

5. BOILED FA*AA*VERGÉ EGGS

"Oh n*ooooooooooooooo*! What h*aa*ave you done??!"

The young Miss Bilke — formerly the Worst Girl Known to Humanity — was relaxing in the warm suds of the turtle bath. She tried to wash around the tag that had been clamped around her ankle, pulling at it, hoping that she could ease it off. No such luck. She had forgotten that she had left something on the hob in the kitchen.

Margaret, who planned to heat up some soup while Agatha bathed, had just noticed the empty pan that had boiled dry. Inside it were three blackened Favergé eggs.

"You cannot boil a jewelled *oeuf*!" she shrieked through the flat. "It is not a real foodstuff! They are worth thousaaands, millions — now destroyed! What *aaa*m I going to do with you??"

Margaret despaired. She threw the eggs in the bin, opened the soup and added a few pickled onions to give it a bit of zing. Why did her sister need so much instruction? Why was she so different from all the other children? She was always getting into trouble.

It was true: Agatha's early upbringing had been both long and arduous for her family. One moment a twinkle in her father's eye, the next a full-throttle, terrorising tomahawk of a girl.

Her parents had decided not to have another child since first-born Margaret seemed intent on eating them out of house and home. They had reasoned — quite understandably — that one child was just about enough, and two would see them bankrupt: no job, no future... no tins of sardines left in the cupboard (and there's usually loads of them if nothing else).

And so Mrs Bilke was surprised when she discovered that she was expecting, and when Agatha had arrived, she had hoped that Margaret, already ten years old, might make a friend soon and go round to their house for tea — just to leave the house for a while and eat someone else's food. They prayed that this new baby would be a calm, kind child — one that perhaps did not like dancing as much as Margaret, who had scuffed most of the skirting boards

They prayed that this new baby would be a calm, kind child...

one that perhaps did not like dancing as much as Margaret, who had scuffed most of the skirting boards and furniture with her inelegant moves

and furniture with her inelegant moves.

But Mrs Bilke, who suffered from nerves as it was, grew disheartened when her new baby would not stop crying. If Margaret tried to help, little Agatha would bash her over the nose. She vomited, cooed, burped and waved her arms in the air like every other child in the world. But she never started smiling and would hardly notice when Mr Bilke pretended to be a monster. She was checked for deafness, short-sightedness and stupidity. She was prodded by a doctor and tickled by a nurse but they found nothing. Baby Agatha was, quite simply, always in a bad mood.

It was only in November of her first year that she perked up. A family trip to the local fireworks display was a big hit. For almost the first time ever, Agatha giggled and laughed, squealed and snorted. She was slightly sick on her new fluffy top and laughed even more. The family bonded; the four of them, living 'n' learning 'n' loving 'n' watching ten tons of explosives zoom off into the night.

It was never quite the same again – the fireworks were the start of a worrying trend. Agatha seemed to be obsessed by the fireplace – and candles. It was around this time that Mr Bilke became a little distant, going out for "coffees" when Mrs Bilke knew that he'd always preferred tea.

Sometimes even Mrs Bilke found it impossible to deal

with her daughter's moods, and found it best to ignore her. Primary school had not improved things: Agatha did not make any friends. She hated the teachers and didn't like schoolwork. And she certainly never acquired any of those typical schoolchild symbols of success: a cabinet full of sports trophies or a wall of certificates. No, Agatha had merely scraped by, and had caused a rumpus in certain other ways. *Bad* ways.

☆ ☆ ☆

It was now, over a decade later, that Margaret Bilke was having to deal with the child. She knew that Agatha needed to be trusted if she was to visit the villa alone tonight. Margaret would have to "chill out", as she'd heard someone say once. As her sister appeared from the bathroom and sat at the kitchen table. she looked apologetic but didn't bother to say sorry. Margaret breathed in, then breathed out again. She dropped her shoulders – until they hunched up again with stress.

The soup was almost entirely disgusting, but they both ate it, slowly and quietly. The smaller, more troublesome Bilke wondered if she should suggest they pop out for fish and chips instead – or perhaps some caviar. Wasn't her sister minted? Or they could skip dinner, buy a yacht and make friends with a movie mogul. Agatha fancied a career in Hollywood (in the remake of *Blazing Saddles* perhaps?). She wondered why Margaret was so irked about a couple of silly eggs, when she could afford a whole Favergé chicken factory – but Bilke the elder had other things on her mind: serious matters.

"Ag*aaa*tha," she said suddenly. "I need you to help me with a little job. I have some troublesome tenants, you see, who need evicting from my luxury vill*aaa*. They are avoiding me – I want you to go and persuade them to move on, yes? P*aaa*ss the *beurre de paysan*, please."

"But I have a tag on… and I want to watch the telly and eat sweets."

"I'm not *aaa*sking you, I'm telling you," barked Margaret. "I'm in big ships if you don't get them the frizz out of my house."

She slammed her silver spoon down on the table, then regained her composure – nothing was won on anger alone (apart from quite a few wars, boxing matches, modelling competitions, scientific discoveries, disputed areas of land etc.) Margaret explained carefully that there was a boy about Agatha's age in the villa, and that he must be the one that she approach first. Agatha would have to use any means

The soup was almost entirely disgusting, but they both ate it, slowly and quietly

to get into the house, even if that meant pretending to be French, Russian or even Chinese. Then she could serve them notice to quit.

"Don't you have security men to do this for you?" Agatha was not pleased at being ordered about: it sounded like a difficult job.

Margaret was becoming irate. She had not expected such resistance from her sister, who had seen how rich and successful she was. She had presumed the luxurious setting would have made her more deferential, not the opposite.

"You're my only hope!" insisted the older Bilke, pressing her sister's forearm in a bothersome way.

"Push off," said Agatha, who wanted to laze around. She'd had a hard time in the last week and she thought that she deserved a rest.

"Sistaaaaaaaaaaa... I need your help..."

"You haven't even asked me about my time at Demone's. It was rubbish. She sat in her room all day looking at her computer..."

"Oh dear. Well anyway, I waaant you to – "

"You haven't listened to a word I've said. You don't care about my time at Demone's!" She got up to leave the table but Margaret grabbed her forearm with her manicured talons and wouldn't let go. She was livid.

"LISTEN TO *ME* for a moment, will you? Have some respect for once! *Aaaa*after all I've done for you..."

The obnoxious child stopped. She realised that if she continued in this vein she could be sent back home, to England.

"Woe is me!" gasped Margaret who just couldn't keep up the fancy-pants act any longer. "OK, Agatha. Let me explain. This ap*aaaa*rtment is... er... not quite what it seems. My – *our* – smart lifestyle is in pieces if you do not go to the villa..."

She looked around her and waved a hand about, melo-dramatically. "I've just had to cancel the driver and limo!" she sniffed. "Soon it will be no more *jus d'éléphant*! Or tur-tle b*aaa*ths! Or yachts in the h*aaa*rbour..." She gazed out of the window, forgetting that there would always be yachts in the harbour, whether she had a high standard of living or not.

"You need to do it tonight, Agatha."

"I see... " her sister replied. "Well, OK, let's make a deal." She was quite level-headed and cunning sometimes, despite being ~~completely out of control~~ a little wayward. If we all remember rightly, she was still dressed like a computer whizz from Brioche in mid-winter.

"If you get me an entire new wardrobe this afternoon, I will help you out."

"But I haaave almost no money!"

Agatha picked up Margaret's swanky handbag. Tassels that had been dipped in an entirely new and expensive type of gold dangled from the pockets; toenails of the great red elephant swung from the zipper and a rare purple squirrel tooth decorated the clasp. She plucked a wodge of euros from the purse inside and spread them out on the table.

"I think this will do."

And so the Bilke girls went shopping.

6. THE POULET VUITTONNE LUXURY LUGGAGE BOUTIQUE

The fashionable rue Contretemps near the seafront was southern France's premier shopping street, lined with swish boutiques and people who looked like they never laughed.

Of course, Agatha had heard the phrase "chic boutique" before but was never entirely sure what this meant – having nothing similar in Rottington; the nearest they had to such a thing was a Primart, which sold cheap clothes that "bobbled" as soon as you put them on.

The *rue* was full of older English women, deep-soaked in sun, with shiny ~~otters~~ cheeks. They were so very thin that they could have been mistaken for giant knitting needles. Agatha was thrilled: high fashion was hers! And *French* high fashion! Just as she had seen in the magazines she used to nick from the newsagent. Just like the girls at Demone's school. She had never before had the lifestyle or the cash, but today was a brand new day in the brand new life of the Most Trendy Girl Known to Humanity.

She spent the afternoon trying on all manner of bizarre outfits. She chose a bright blue frock from Jim Galliani which had a small waist and a wide skirt. She picked out a pair of Diorgh python-skin platform shoes to match. They clashed with her tag — a fact which the enthusiastic boutique owner thought was "divine". The hat she chose resembled a plate of breaded scampi.

"Zat is *fantastique!*" squealed the shop owner, who put false eyelashes on her and painted her nails a vile shade of green, which Ag thought rather fetching.

Their last stop was the Poulet Vuittonne Luxury Luggage Boutique, as Margaret wanted a status-enhancing keyring, to reward herself for such a long afternoon. As soon as Agatha saw the purses, she demanded one — wearing brand new clothes was not enough. She decided on a wallet which was made out of gerbil skin, and cost over ten thousand euros. Margaret said no, as she made her own purchase.

"Why can't I have the purse?" raged Agatha, who had been sucked in by a consumerist whirl (which was quite

The hat she chose resembled a plate of breaded scampi

pleasant and it gave her a buzzy feeling in the back of her ears). "I want it."

"That's not the point," countered Margaret. "You've haaaad lots of presents today. You must go and wrestle my property baaack for me now."

"I can't be bothered."

"Aaaagatha, you must. I haaave just spent a lot of money on you."

"You don't care if I live or die!"

Margaret gave the Poulet staff a look. One which suggested a life of infinite pain and unending misery.

As Agatha was dragged from the shop she swiped an mp3 cover (which cost hundreds) right from under the shop assistants' noses. They ran after the pair but were left behind when Margaret hailed a taxi.

"Ooohhgh! I can never go in there again!" wailed Margaret in the cab. "I'm dropping you off at the Villa de Mer immediately! You must now fulfil your half of the bargain!"

The cab took a few minutes to arrive at the mansion. It gave Agatha time to think. Of course, she did not like being bullied by her sister, but

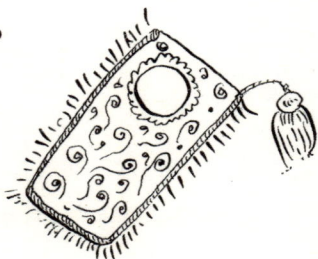

wasn't this a bit of an adventure? Who knows what sort of people she might meet in there? In her new clothes she could pretend to be a bottom-kicking landlord, a real heavyweight. It would be practice for her future role as a property millionaire. She was rather excited, but tried not to show it.

When they reached the front gates, Bilke senior stopped the cab and elbowed her out onto the road.

"We're here. Get my estate b*aaa*ck for me, or you go b*aaa*ck to Rottington!"

She thrust an envelope with her last 20 euros into Agatha's hand, to pay for the taxi journey back to the flat.

"The eviction papers, sis. Now do your ~~worst~~ best!!"

7. THE FAMILY OF "LE MONSIEUR"

Dressed like a merry parakeet on a bank holiday, Agatha Bilke walked up to the extravagant rental property. The driveway was lined with palm trees and passion flower bushes – the building itself was low but obviously roomy. Soft music – a recorder? – was playing from somewhere inside and many of the lights were on. This was a balmy summer evening, and birds sang as she walked along the gravel. She clutched the envelope in her hand and inhaled slowly.

The palms, so common to this part of France, suddenly ceased at the front of the house. In their place, there was a rose bush, a rope ladder, a well and a small vegetable plot. There were wellington boots by the door and a large bow and arrow – which appeared to be crafted out of rubber bands and sticks. Was this a family home or was it a meeting place for the boy scouts? Agatha could hear faint voices coming from the house and her confidence faltered. Who or what would she find inside?

Margaret had failed to say whether the family were French, English or otherwise. Were they aggressive or mild-mannered; executive types or layabouts? Agatha had been provided with no detail whatsoever. Maybe they all had beards – even the kids – and had spent all their money on special clippers and shampoos. Maybe they would kill her, because she was beardless.

As she was contemplating running away and joining the circus, the door opened. Agatha wished she didn't have the false eyelashes on – they were making it difficult for her to see properly.

A child of about ten, wearing shorts and a v-necked jumper, appeared. His knees were scuffed and dirty.

"*Bonjour.*" He smirked as he looked her up and down.

"Erm, *bonjour.* Could I talk with the rent dodgers, *s'il vous plaît?*" Agatha adopted a stern pose (hands on hips) which showed that she was on serious business. After all, she mustn't let a young boy put her off.

"Come in, *Mademoiselle...*"

This fellow did not seem to register Agatha's authoritarian

manner. He sloped down the palatial hall and disappeared into a room somewhere. Agatha had no idea whether she should follow or not. She stood for a moment and heard laughing, shouting and giggling – unfamiliar noises for someone who had so recently been cooped up in Demone's bedroom watching her use Instant Messenger all day.

Agatha looked around her. What had once been a beautiful home was now admittedly a bit of a mess. The walls were daubed with paint splodges and badly put-up shelves. There was loud banging coming from one part of the house.

She set off along the corridor shouting, "*Excuse me! I have a notice to quit this property!*" but no one bothered to listen. She glanced into one of the rooms. A girl of about her age was reclining on a sofa, reading a comic. In the next room a group of kids were playing marbles and squealing with delight.

Agatha walked into the impressive kitchen area to see kids baking cakes, giggling as they ate some of the uncooked mixture. No one took any notice of her. A phone upstairs kept ringing. It remained unanswered.

She stepped outside into the garden to see a great treehouse. Children from six to sixteen sat, high above the ground, drinking lemonade – not the clear, fizzy sort that

Agatha was used to, but proper, *home-made* cloudy lemonade with bits in. One little boy swung dreamily back and forth in a tyre swing. Along the bottom of the garden ran a stream. Children were fishing – some paddling in the clear water. A boy whizzed past her, shouting to his friends: "Hey! I've found the pin-hole camera!"

Most of the kids were talking in English; all appeared to be content. They looked like they came from a mix of backgrounds and cultures. If this was a family, it was a very big family. No wonder Margaret couldn't get them out.

☆ ☆ ☆

What struck Agatha was that this was something she had never before encountered – children having fun. Back in the mists of time, "fun" for Agatha Bilke had mainly involved matches and large buildings. This scene was idyllic. The oddest thing of all, she noticed, was that there was no TV and no computer – everyone was smiling, enjoying the simple things in life.

"Look, friends! It's a gramophone player!" A tall boy had found a contraption from one of the rooms and wheeled it outside onto the grass. The children gathered around as he opened the built-in cupboard below, pulled out a 78 rpm

One little boy swung dreamily back and forth in a tyre swing

disc, and placed it on the turntable.

"Wind it up, little Chi-Du!" he cried to the small boy next to him. A fast-paced samba simmered from the one speaker and everyone cheered.

Although this hideaway was in France, Agatha could have been right back in Rottington – in the 1950s, that is. But this did not worry her. For a girl who had just come from the world of virtual geeks and cyber bullies, square eyes and microwave lasagne, the whole thing was entrancing and all notions of evicting the children vanished. Forget Margaret and her egg collection! She wanted to become part of the group. She would forgo all her past hobbies; no more texting the man from the supermarket, claiming to have planted a bomb by the kippers. Agatha stood in the corner, gazing in wonder. She scrunched up the letter in her hand and made a big decision: she would not serve them notice to quit. With no bin in sight, she stuffed the paper in her jacket pocket and forgot about it.

The jolly atmosphere was shattered by a voice on the speaker system.

"*Mes chatons furieux!*" cried a boy's voice in broken French. "Inside now. We have an intruder!"

Les chatons? Agatha was baffled by the name. And who or what was running the show?

8. THE FURIOUS KITTENS

Each and every child ran into the house. Metal grilles automatically descended over the windows to secure them all inside. A siren wailed and ~~horses~~ hoses began to water the grass. A not-so-concealed camera spun around, trying to capture an image of the visitor.

Agatha dashed under the lowering barricades and rolled into safety. Inside, the lights had been switched off and the same boy's voice was making a speech. Agatha spotted the kitchen table and dived under it. She listened with all ears (of which she had two).

"My furious kittens..."

So this is what the name meant!

"...If we are going to be so lax as to let a complete stranger into the house," the voice continued, "I will have to go through the rules again with you."

The voice was firm, most definitely angry. The children gulped. Agatha gulped.

"The first rule of *les chatons* is that we do not allow anyone into the house. The *second* rule is that we do not allow anyone into the house. The third rule" – Agatha had not guessed this one – "is that we *may* let someone in if they are good at rafting or making knots and they don't want to evict us. At least we have installed those metal grilles to protect us. The visitor should be long-gone now."

"Ah *oui*, Le Monsieur!" cried the crowd, who seemed more relaxed now. They were pleased that "the intruder" had disappeared and did not stop to think that she might be inside among them, getting pins and needles under a table.

Who was *Le Monsieur*? He spoke in an English accent yet had a French name. Agatha had already realised that this was not a traditional family, but she now saw that it was even more unusual that she'd first thought.

"Followers, it's been a difficult week," the voice continued. "We have managed to stay in the villa despite constant haranguing from our dreadful landlady."

Agatha strained to look out from under the table – this made her pins and needles worse. She could not see the speaker, but caught a glimpse of a dartboard on the far wall, which – *ugh* – had a picture of Margaret and several hundred holes in it.

"We must fight, my kittens, for what we believe in!" continued Le Monsieur. "I have a dream! That we are living the perfect childhood in our unending summer camp – no one can stop us or our passion for traditional childish pastimes! *What-ho!*"

Every kitten cheered. The mood had been elevated and Agatha marvelled at the charismatic leader. He had the children eating out of the palm of his hand – and when he picked up the freshly baked biscuits and tossed them into the crowd it proved the point.

Hang on... there was something familiar about him – Agatha couldn't quite pinpoint what it was. Hm...

"*What-ho!*"

The words rung in her head like a ~~particularly wriggly octopus~~ loud bell.

In the silence, as happy followers munched their snacks, she remembered who he was: Holbeck Folbeck, her old friend whom she'd left for dead at the Rottington hospital (well, nearly). The tiny [tiny] speck of heart inside her started leaping. It *was* him! That posh way of talking – the *by crikeys* and of course the *what-hos*. The fun they'd had together! The hilarious, if not a little dangerous, times they'd shared. And now, the pair had been flung together again by fate! She was delighted. That said, he was now a cult leader and she looked like a psychedelic goat. Would they ever be friends again?

A piercing sound interrupted the calm. "*Tweeeerping! Tweeeerping!*"

Agatha's tag. It was past curfew and she needed to be at home with her sister.

"*Tweeeerping! Tweeeerping!*"

Le Monsieur was flummoxed.

"What's that noise? Is the intruder still here? Come out, stranger, whoever you are!"

Everyone started looking for the source of the noise. Agatha cowered: what would they do with her once she had been discovered? Chain her to a wooden hop and stick set? Plonk her up in the treehouse until she starved? Play dominoes with her day and night until she crumbled?

The tag still shrieked and she sat undetected. Crikey, these children were hopeless; they couldn't even see her lime-green platform shoes sticking out from under the table. After ten minutes of wondering if her legs were going to seize up, Agatha decided that enough was enough and poked her head out.

"Here I am!" she announced. "The intruder! But don't

"We must fight, my kittens, for what we believe in!"
continued Le Monsieur

worry, I am going to leave now, thanks."

Le Monsieur barred the way. Close up, she could see that he was wearing a wig.

"You cannot go: the place is sealed." He looked her up and down. "What was that bleeping noise? A secret spy camera? A mobile phone? Tell us who you work for now!"

A small boy of about seven, in lederhosen, sidled up and tried to look threatening, but he failed.

"It's a police tag." admitted Agatha. The leader softened.

"Ah!" he exclaimed, and looked nostalgic. "I had one of those, years ago! Different design, mind, but – what-ho! – such a laugh! May I ask your name, young *mademoiselle*?"

Agatha had to think fast. "Fifi le Feu," she said.

"Welcome!" Holbeck stretched out his arms.

"You're home now, with your people. *Pierre*!" he shouted, as a teenage boy rushed towards him.

"Take the tag off this young lady, make sure she has a hot bath and…" He turned to "Fifi". "Um – have you got any *practical* clothes?"

Agatha looked blank.

"Never mind, eh, by *jiminee*?" His breath smelt of mints – it was Holby, most definitely. "Might actually work in your favour."

With a crowbar, Pierre cut the tag and smashed it up

with a loud "voilà!". Then he picked up his book on Lenny Mailer and continued reading. What a macho, literary type, thought many of the young girls there.

"Come up to the ballroom once you're refreshed, Fifi," said Le Monsieur. He smiled like a crow who's just spotted a nice juicy worm.

9. HOLBECK

It was Margaret's fault, thought Agatha. She must have known all along that Holbeck was holed up here, and had taken advantage of her younger sister. But now the errant girl in platform shoes would turn out to be Margaret's worst nightmare: she was not only refusing to evict the group, she was going to join them. Her elder sister's superiority was short-lived — had it lasted even an afternoon? Agatha would always get one over her sister. Fancy wanting to make a houseful of innocent children homeless! What a nerve!

As she undressed — it was her second hot bath of the day but she felt obliged to take it — Agatha felt smug. And then the grin fell from her face like an amateur mountaineer slipping off Ben Nevis. How should she play it with Holby?

She desperately wanted him to recognise her behind all the haute couture. She wanted them to relive the heady days of the hospital. But she couldn't reveal her identity, not yet. He must be in a lot of trouble, with no money to pay the rent and no parents to support him. She should find out more about his situation before she risked showing him who she was – apart from anything else, harking back to the old days would be a distraction, and Holbeck clearly needed to concentrate all his current efforts on sorting his problems out.

She heard the phone ringing again and this time Le Monsieur picked up the receiver. She strained to hear the conversation.

"Darnnit! Eh? Ah, little Albert is fine... And no, you can't speak to him at the present time. He is – um – doing some sums. Yes, yes, we will get back to you tomorrow. I must bid you good day. No... no, Monsieur Citron, everything is under control here. Hey, do not call me names! I am a respectable boy! Bonsoir!"

He slammed the phone down.

The truth was that Agatha could not have begun to imagine what a mess Holbeck was in.

The Villa de Mer was being used as a summer camp. When his parents had left at the end of spring, Holbeck had needed to raise some cash for the rent. He had placed an advert in the local press announcing a place for "all kids under sixteen" to have fun in the holidays and learn English at the same time. He had promised it would be "very educational" and that he, Le Monsieur, was highly trained. He had been a victim of his own success. Once the children got there and found no lessons and no real discipline, they never wanted to leave. Holbeck had accidentally created the perfect environment where they could be free to run around. More children joined and he could not get rid of the first lot. Now the parents were starting to wonder when their offspring were coming back. Holbeck was torn – should he urge the children to go home, or keep them there? Perhaps he would be able to make the parents cough up for "extra tuition"... And yet the longer the children stayed, the more suspicious he became of anyone infiltrating the group – which is why he hadn't answered the door to Margaret when she had visited. And let's face it, no parent in their right mind was really going to hand over more cash to enable their child to continue at the mysterious villa. He had to find money to pay the rent now. Himself.

Why did he not simply leave the Villa de Mer? Ensure the parents picked up their children and have done with it? Because, strange though it may seem, Holbeck had grown fond of his followers... there was little Chi-Du who was not sleeping well at night. And young Pliny with that terrible bunion on her toe. The children relied on him and he was protective. Ultimately, he wanted to escape the emotional and financial burden, but he found he just couldn't say no. And he certainly did not want to go back to his parents and... whisper it... boarding school.

☆ ☆ ☆

The villa was enormous, with oak panelling in some rooms, pictures of aristocrats everywhere and vast chandeliers that you could have mistaken for ~~motorbikes~~ planets were they not inside a house. It took Agatha a while to locate the ballroom. It was almost like walking into a James Bund film set, although everyone was a lot younger – and there were fewer cars. The leader was surrounded by a small group of children who looked at him, besotted, as he spoke to the new arrival.

"You join us just as a big change is taking place," said the furious kittens' boss. "I have just had word from a source in Paris. I may have some, erm, business to attend to in the capital."

What? She had just found him — and now he was leaving her! Agatha really did like the boy and was astounded they had met up again under such odd circumstances. She *had* to remain with him now that they were together again.

"I have a question to ask," said Holbeck. "Pardon me for being direct, but Fifi, do you have any spare cash? You've got a lot of very expensive clothes on and so I thought you might be able to... um. ." he trailed off.

"Sorry, Le Monsieur," said "Fifi". I have nothing left; I am poor." She drooped her head slightly so that he might feel sorry for her. He didn't

"Dash it to frizz!" The enigmatic leader was agitated. Agatha wanted to reach out and mop his posh brow but she couldn't let her persona slip. She must retain her cool.

"My 'family' is special to me," he said. "We *Chatons* are all waifs and strays. We want to stay together... no one bossing us about, no restrictions, no bedtime. But we are broke. I've come to the end of my allowance. Mater and Pater are on their uppers. If *you* have no money then I will have to go and plead with the, erm, embassy."

Words started spilling out of Agatha, as if she was a typewriter that had been sat on by a very fat rhinoceros.

"Let me help! I will come with you to Paris! I have a lot of ingenuity and at least I *look* like I've got money." It wasn't the most romantic of sentiments, but it did the job.

"Well, I might need someone to carry my briefcase, yes..." He was thinking hard.

"I'll come with you too!" squeaked an acolyte, and then another. Holbeck had to explain that he needed people back here to "hold the fort – *eh, by crikey!* – and that sort of thing". The fewer of their number who went, he explained, the more likely they were to secure the dosh. He bent his head to the left and looked at Agatha.

"You're very familiar, Fifi... Did we meet at Clichy? Or perhaps the avenue du Soleil in Monaco last year?"

"I don't think so," said Agatha. When she was alone with him she could tell him the truth. Paris! It would be a dream come true.

"It won't be *all* hard slog." He came up closer to her. "We'll squat in a swanky apartment until the moolah comes through. Then I may have a small cognac and we can try our hand at poetry. We can come back here in due course and build a wooden octopus for the garden, which the kids all seem to be hankering after..."

"I don't know anything about Paris," said Agatha, frankly.

"Oh, let me be the one to show you! The cafés, the boulevards, the revolutionary zeal... the, um, tiny dogs!" replied Holbeck. "It will be a blast."

10. TROUBLE

Margaret had left Agatha to deal with the Folbecks and knew that it might take a while, but now it was almost midnight and, sitting in her luxury apartment with a leaky turtle bath, she was a little anxious.

Was she taking her time because the family had asked her to help them pack? Perhaps they had made her stay for supper when they found out what a good friend she was of their son. (Margaret had no idea how much Mrs Folbeck hated young Agatha.) She wondered whether she should go over there herself – but she had given up the limo and had no more cash left for a taxi. She reasoned that Agatha would be all right, because she was a resilient type, and she'd see her some time soon.

By morning, however, she was ~~anxiouser~~ even more

anxious. She considered the possibilities. No answer, as usual, on the telephone number of the villa. Maybe she had gone back to Demone's — having forgotten a favourite pen or her pyjamas. No, this wasn't right — something was amiss. She decided to email the French exchange.

To: Canard, Demone <demone.canard@bebois.com>
From: Bilke, Margaret <property.tycoon@tycoonyfeelings.net>
Time: 08.04 CET

Subject: Mlle Agatha

Hiya Dermonnne. It's Margaret Bilke, the sister d'Agatha here. Do you know where Agatha est? I cannot find her and I've looked for her everywhere. She even has a tag but she's missing! Is she back with you and your Canards?

All my amours,

Margaret

To: Bilke, Margaret <property.tycoon@tycoonyfeelings.net>
From: Canard, Demone <demone.canard@bebois.com>

Time: 08.08 CET
Subject: Re: Mlle Agatha

Hey Ciao Margarets. I haven't viewed Agatha for a long times now, yes. If I will see her I hates her, she ruins my reputation with videos inside a Bebois.com and the frogs hurt. I am blinded by legs! If I finds her first, the since is soonest, I gives her a piece of my minds.
Best wishing and sinceres,
Demone

Margaret did not understand all of the reply and was perturbed. It did not sound as if Agatha was with Demone. Where could she be? Her little sister had been missing for a day now.

Of course! The tag! Perhaps it had gone off and the police had found her and taken her into custody. How stupid she had been to gamble with such a contraption. *Frizz.* She rang the gendarmes – it took ages to get through. When she did speak to someone they had never heard of Agatha; let alone taken her to the station. Margaret was not happy. Everything was going wrong.

"I presume you *caaaa*n locate her," she shrieked. "Her

taaag must be bleeping away!"

The woman on the other end of the phone told her to hang on, then went away for twenty minutes.

"Zorry, *Madame*. We 'ave looked at ze computer and we 'ave no communicazions wiv zis tag. Are you sure she 'ad one fitted?"

"Yes, yes!" cried Margaret, who was now 100% irate, as opposed to being 98% irate and 2% sensible a minute ago. "You should arrest *yourselves* because you *aaaa*re full of incompetence!"

She slammed the phone down, and in doing so knocked an ornamental lizard off the base.

Margaret Bilke decided there was nothing else for it but to walk to the Villa de Mer and try and retrieve Agatha herself. She must be there – perhaps accidentally fallen down the well or stuck up a palm tree.

☆ ☆ ☆

It took an hour and her feet hurt by the time she got to the mansion. She sighed despairingly as she saw what a mess had been made of the front garden. The place looked ruined – old sticks, boots and mixing bowls were strewn over the grass. The windows had all been left open and the lights on.

"Is there *aaaa*nybody in there?" she called. There was no reply.

Margaret tried the door – it too was open. She walked in and what she saw was horrifying. She had last been in the property when it was new and clean, with Mrs Folbeck running her fingers along the dado rail to check for dust.

There was debris everywhere: cake tins, poster paints, huge dressing-up boxes and, in the garden, a treehouse made out of her valuable Louis XIV furniture. There were tyre-marks over the walls where someone had tried to ride a bicycle. And – *oh no!* – in the centre of the living room a dartboard with her face on it. Sobbing, she went upstairs. In the middle of the ballroom floor lay proof that Agatha Bilke was gone – her yellow tag, broken into a thousand pieces (or even more).

What had happened? Could the Folbeck family have done this?

Margaret had no knowledge of Holbeck's summer camp – the fact that so many children had been living in the villa without adult supervision. She would never have guessed that Agatha and Holbeck had gone early that morning. They had left the children to look after themselves, although in fact they had fled soon afterwards – which was not part of Holbeck's plan. If Margaret had been aware of any of this, she would have wondered where they had gone. It will be left for us, dear reader, to ask that question ourselves.

☆ ☆ ☆

Demone Canard sat at home. This was interesting – so Agatha had a tag! This meant that if the computer geek could hack her way into the central police computer she should be able to find out where her "friend" was. She wanted to even the score. Agatha had made fun of her and it would not do. The girl spent a few minutes getting through the system with elaborate passwords and some fancy decoding until, at last, she had access to the "Surveillance" section. (This was much more than the local policewoman could do, when Margaret had phoned the station. So many of these officials were useless with computers!) Demone started filling in the blanks on screen, tapping in her enemy's name and details:

Perpetrator de crime: <u>Agatha Bilke</u>
Tag: <u>Plastique, Yellow</u>

She waited a few moments and the following appeared on screen:

Location: La Villa de Mer

Then:

ERROR MESSAGE! ERROR MESSAGE!
Malfunction avec tag: le code 674998
ERROR MESSAGE! ERROR MESSAGE!

Where could the English girl be? Demone saw that Agatha had left her copy of *Compliment Bonjour* by the computer and tried to flick through the gluey pages, only to find the word "Paris" circled on the back cover. Aha! This surely meant that she had gone there!

Demone logged in to her own online bank account and saw that she still had a lot of cash from the time she had

hacked into La Banque de Mayonnaise and moved a few thousand euros from a stranger's current account into her own, just for a laugh.

She grabbed a coat and ran for the railway station to board the next train to the Gare de Lyon. She would find Agatha if it was the last thing she did. With Mademoiselle Canard's technological know-how she knew she could track her down.

11. PABLO PICASSO

"Le Monsieur" was nervous. Agatha wondered if he wouldn't just pass out from the strain when he arrived. On the train to Paris he had fidgeted, bitten his nails, ground his teeth and picked things out of his ear. He drank four coffees, two teas (and sipped from what looked like a secret flagon of brandy), ate nine "Nuttington" chocolate bars, a Folbecks' Imperial D'elurge and then was sick out of the window. All of which he didn't want "Fifi" to notice, but she did anyway. What was he so fearful of? He must have needed the money more urgently than she imagined.

Walking out of the station, Agatha was captivated. Paris was like a postcard – filled with images she had seen in films and on the telly, enlarged and illuminated – real and

Paris was like a postcard – real and unreal

unreal. It was almost exactly as she had pictured it. The main streets were wide and lined with trees. There were newspaper kiosks on every corner and tiny dogs' as Holbeck had promised – they wore little coats. They passed smaller, winding streets with tiny shops selling watches and lampshades; jewellery and jams.

She had never witnessed such style and, in the people, such confidence – everyone walked with a swagger. The women sashayed along the road and seemed a million miles away from the ladies of Rottington Town. They had gusto, they had grace – *and* looked liked they read a load of books. The men were dashing, mysterious and they too appeared to be thinking about Important Stuff. They spoke a charming language, musical and sweet.

"Blah blah, croissant beurre blanc, Sartre, Camus, cinema intellectuel, et j'aime les politiques serieux non?"

"Ah oui – blah blah Picasso, Flaubert, je suis très good-looking et j'aime les Arts aussi et je wearing mon Yves Saint Lemone jacket, d'accord."

It was nothing like Brioche or Cannes. The Parisians were a breed apart.

Her attention turned to Le Monsieur who was still muttering to himself. *"Le Tour Eiffel, L'Arc de Triomphe, Musée du Louvre, the Champs Elysées, the Mona Lisa..."* Holbeck's cheeks were flushed, but he thought that reeling off this list of tourist attractions would be an ideal way to calm his jitters. He was attempting to instruct Fifi in all things Parisian, as she had claimed not to know anything about the place.

"Put simply, Mademoiselle le Feu, the French have always been a warring nation: the capital's history is about the people's struggle. The Parisii were one of the first tribes to make their home in the Ile de la Cité but when the Romans invaded they were allowed to remain. Did you know they called it Lutetia? Very interesting. Then we get to the golden age of kings and stuff in the late eighteenth century... the working classes didn't like King Louis XVI, so he and the missus were executed. Then there was the Commune which was a bit of a racy idea as the People governed the People, but they overthrew *that* too. In the 1920s

There were tiny dogs, as Holbeck had promised

it was all jazz clubs and people taking their clothes off; then the Second World War; the Nazi occupation; and in '68 some students rioting about bin bags – or was that punk? – and now us! Fifi and Le Monsieur! I wonder where we'll fit in?" Agatha was not paying much attention to the posh boy's lecture. She was still listening in on other people's conversations and in particular, a crowd of geeky-looking computer fans, gathering outside Le Dejeuner Sur L'Herbe internet café, waiting for it to open. A few words were familiar:

"Blah blah, wois wois Demone Canard blah blah wois wois she is on the internet et looking for Agatha et revonge!"

"All I need do is schedule a meeting with my business partner this afternoon," continued Holbeck, blithely. "And then we can be back by nightfall. You will have to help me, Fifi. Oh and I mentioned all that stuff about taking an apartment and what-have-you, but I think we should just return to our HQ at the Villa de Mer, *eh what?*

"*Shhhhh!*" whispered Agatha and stopped walking.

"Eh? By crikey, girl, there's no need to be rude."

"I'm sorry, I just need you to translate for me. What are they saying? What does '*revonge*' mean?" Agatha was vexed – it was clear that someone was talking about Demone Canard.

Holbeck stopped his chatter. He listened but did not seem overly concerned.

"'Revonge'...? Must be revenge, but a really *devastating* sort. It's nothing, Fifi," smiled Holbeck, his wig drooping a little to the right. "Just about some girl who wants to wreak an utterly dreadful attack on someone called Agatha. No one we know of."

"Le Monsieur, are you short-sighted?" At the Rottington Agatha remembered that he had worn a monocle. Now, half blind, he had no idea who she really was.

"Erm... yes. I suppose I should really put my glasses on." He fumbled around in his pockets but was having difficulty. "I know I put them somewhere..."

He continued up the road, screwing up his eyes, looking at the building numbers, chewing his fingernails. Away from his home, he hardly seemed the leader of an exciting band of wayward children (wherever they were). He was quieter, less exciting. Agatha wondered exactly what she had got herself into.

12. RUDOLPHE CITRON

Some time later that same day, down in the South of France, Monsieur Citron arrived at the Villa de Mer, which was now home to a small claw of pigeons (if that is the collective term) due to the fact that the last person to leave had forgotten to lock the door behind them. He searched each and every room for signs of his son, Albert Citron, a small child who was fond of wearing lederhosen, and soon became distressed when he realised that there was no one there at all.

The proud father had been suspicious of the Villa de Mer for a while now. The camp Albert had joined for the summer holidays had not operated as he had expected it to. He had a feeling that his letters had been intercepted and he had only got through on the telephone once, despite trying several times. He had spoken to a guy called "Le Monsieur" who'd told him off for letting his boy watch too much telly at home, then informed him that the child did not want to return. Le Monsieur mentioned something about aliens landing and then cut him off. This wasn't normal.

The lack of children, and of "Le Monsieur", was worrying. They might have been on an educational day-trip to the seaside, but Rudolphe Citron just didn't think so. The pigeons were busy pecking at some left-over pastries. Which was not very nice to watch.

It was only when Monsieur Citron glanced over at the table where the yukky birds sat, that he noticed one of them eating not a *pain au raisin* but a piece of paper. The man waved his hands about to frighten the creature and seized the sheet. On it were noted the times of coach journeys to Paris, plus a scrawled message: *cherchez Le Monsieur!*

Monsieur Citron heard footsteps along the hallway. A woman who introduced herself as Madame Bovary walked in. She was tall with bright red hair.

"Are you ze looking for your children too?" she asked.

"Yes!" he cried, relieved to find someone in the same boat. "Look at ze mess!"

"I 'ave a daughter 'ere." Bovary was still hopeful. "Perhaps she is hiding upstairs...?"

M. Citron waved his hands about to frighten the creatures

Citron passed her the paper with the coach details. She was horrified that Pliny Bovary could have gone so far, but pleased that she might have a chance of finding her. There was only one thing for it: she must go up to Paris herself.

"I will go up too!" said Rudolphe. "What about ze other kiddiwinks?"

Madame Bovary and Monsieur Citron started to contact their friends who also had children staying at the camp. Speedily, the parents assembled a small team together and prepared for a trip north. They would catch this villain, Le Monsieur — he had taken their children! It was more than any of them could comprehend and they resolved to act immediately.

13. SNIPPEZ ET SNIPPÉ, THE LAWYERS

There are some well-established ways to get money: grovelling, pretending to be ill, pleading mental instability, wearing lots of make-up (if you're a woman – and maybe if you're not) etc. Holbeck's thinking was just as elaborate and in this instance, "Fifi" in all her finery was integral to his plan.

As they reached the office of Messieurs Snippez et Snippé, the best law firm in France (or so Holbeck had been told by his father), Agatha noticed him acting even more strangely. He started simpering. He spotted a flower stall and bought his companion a red rose. He complimented Agatha on her style and promised he would take her to the opera after the whole "sorry mess" was concluded. He was charming and attentive – but not in a genuine way. What did he want? What was he compensating for? Agatha knew Holbeck well enough to be suspicious about his behaviour.

The lawyers' offices were fusty and dusty. There were ~~flies~~ files everywhere and a pair of desks complete with quills and ink pots, which were so bulky they almost looked like lecterns that a vicar would preach from.

First they met Monsieur Snippez. He was a small man who smelt of damp. He tried to talk to the children polite-ly, but addressed Holbeck as if he was five years old. He brightly explained that he had worn a hat to the office today, and now his hair was as flat as "le pancake".

"Eh! Le hat hair! Heh hehehe-heheh!" he laughed, as the English chil-dren sat, stony-faced.

At this point Monsieur Snippé appeared – another small man who looked exactly like Snippez except that he had a moustache. He frowned for a minute or two, then flicked through a pile of papers on his desk.

Agatha assumed that Holbeck would courteously ask for some money, fresh from his parents' bank account, and that would be that. But it was not quite so simple.

"Gentlemen," Holbeck said, "as you know, I have been residing in my parents' rented villa for six months now. I am at my wits' end. They have abandoned me and I have no funds to keep up the rent payments. I have no food to eat, nothing to drink but water from the stream – and I am all alone. Or rather, I *was*."

The boy reached out for Agatha's hand and looked dotingly at her.

"If *money* iz what you've come for," interrupted Snippez, "Zen you know, *my little oignon*, zat you have come to ze wrong place. We have given you an allowance, zen allowance *plus*, zen part of your inheritance and zen more money to tide you over when you had the Incident with ze Bear."

"Mongolia is a very unforgiving place," said the boy.

"I have to zay, Monsieur, that you've had enough. Mr and Mrs Folbeck are not ze prepared to give you any more money. We cannot do any more. Well, I can show you my pancake hair again, heheheheheh!" Monsieur Snippé growled at the children.

"But this time, my good men, the case is different." Holbeck had prepared his speech. "I suppose you have been enchanted by the ravishing beauty that sits beside me. A mirage, a vision, a fountain of loveliness! Is she real, or perhaps a figment of our wildest fantasies? She even wears designer clothes!"

"Erm, well —" Snippez looked coy and Snippé looked doubtful.

Messieurs Snippez et Snippé

"I can tell you now, from the bottom of my heart —" and it was here that Holbeck stood up on his chair and shouted

— loudly — to Agatha's immense embarrassment: "This is the girl I love!" and to Agatha: *"Fifi le Feu, will you be my wife?"*

Holbeck continued his preposterous speech to the French men in suits: "We are going to be engaged! Then get married when we are older, but honestly, chaps, I've found the lady for me and that being so could I ask you for, say, a million euros? More if Mater and Pater have got it, of course. Mummy always said I would be given a large amount of money if I married the right girl. Here she is! Heh!"

He sat down, like a wasp that's eaten a box of chocolates — feeling a bit sick and buzzy. "They have the funds. I *know*."

Agatha was aghast. Holbeck wanted to marry her! But no, he didn't — he wanted to *tell* everyone he was engaged to the fictional Fifi so he could get what he wanted. He didn't care about her. It was too obvious, too ridiculous — and he was far too young. Agatha was outraged, angry, furious and miffed.

Agatha stood up, like she'd never stood up before.

"Stop! This is a sham!" she cried. "I am not Fifi le Feu. I came here out of curiosity and perhaps that is my mistake. We are *not* going to get married — in six years' time or twenty!"

The lawyers stayed calm, and handed a sheet of paper to Holbeck.

"We are glad *vous êtes ici, Le Monsieur*." Snippé stressed the last two words and the boy turned white: they must have known about the summer camp. "We were forewarned by your parents," continued the man, "that if you came here for money then we should see that you were adequately punished. There is nothing else for it; we must hand you over to be looked after by the French Legal System.

Holbeck blenched. He knew he had no defence. His kittens had been willing participants in his little dream, but they were just *children*; innocents in all of this. He had betrayed their parents' trust, and taken their money on false pretences... This was it – he was going into an institution! The very thought of it.

The men handed him some papers to sign.

"This document means you agree to your incarceration," said Snippé. "And you *must* agree. Now please, do not sign as 'Le Monsieur'..."

Master Folbeck scrabbled for his glasses again but could not find them. Snippé handed him a monocle – similar to the one, Agatha noted. that the boy had worn when she had first met him in Rottington General.

Holbeck turned to Fifi. "Er... Ey! What...!"

Of course, he could now see properly. "Bilky! By crikey!" His surprise turned almost immediately to embarrassment. "Oh, I apologise! I truly do! To get you caught up in this... *sorry mess*. Oh goodness... erm, ah! Ha? Hmmm. Let me explain..."

Agatha was still outraged, no matter how much Holbeck tried to talk his way out of it. She stormed out of the lawyers' office, letting out a stream of furious abuse. ~~Well, it never was long before that happened.~~

"You vile, selfish boy! You cannot toy with people's emotions. You cannot force them to play along with you! I am off – I need a very strong cup of coffee! PS, I HATE YOU!"

Holbeck threw his wig on the ground and stamped on it, ineffectively. He could not do anything right. It was just like his mother said.

☆ ☆ ☆

Unfortunately, while making her dramatic exit from the building, Agatha had made a fatal error. In her swift about-turn, she had dislodged the eviction notice that was stuffed in her inside jacket pocket and it had fallen to the floor. Holbeck picked it up and read: a notice to quit the property – from Margaret Bilke!

Of course, she was Agatha's older sister! This meant that Agatha – *crikey* – had been sent to fish him out of his beloved villa. By frizz! What a two-faced toad of a girl!

Agatha had lied and cheated to get what she wanted. This was too much.

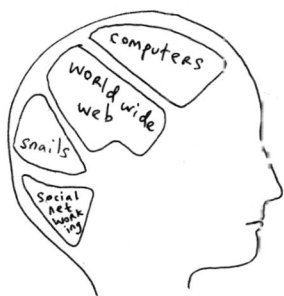

DEMONE'S MIND

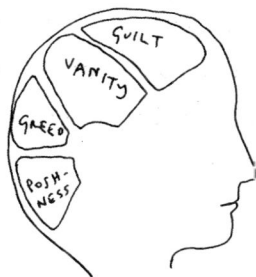

HOLBECK'S MIND

14. IF YOU WERE FEELING GENEROUS

Bound for Paris, Margaret sat back in her plane seat (bought with a credit card already groaning with debt) and thought about the young girl who shared most of her DNA. It had been a short but eventful life thus far. Agatha had irritated the frizz out of everyone, but surely at bottom she had a good heart? Actually, she had no heart at all — that's what the doctors at the Rottington had said. But she had a good... no, she didn't have a good anything. There wasn't a thing you could say about Agatha that didn't include the words "deliberate fire", "nasty" or — if you were feeling generous — "troublesome". It was such a shame.

Of course, Margaret did not blame herself for her sibling's difficult behaviour. She had been gentle and loving, always ready to listen. With such a large age gap between them, there had been points when the girls' paths did not cross for days, weeks, months... but *if* she had ever been called upon to help, she certainly would have done what she could. Mr and Mrs Bilke were always arguing – maybe *their* behaviour had made a difference.

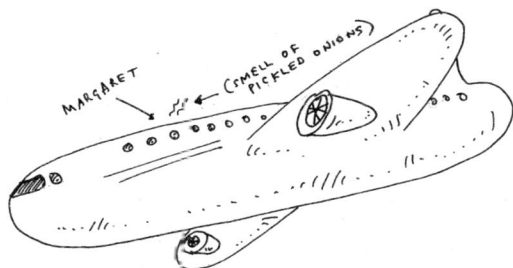

We have already discussed the lack of trophies/good bits in Agatha's early life, but glossed over the specifics. Ahem. Aged four, Agatha had liked to set fire to the wings of butterflies. Aged five, she'd extracted eight teeth from a schoolfriend (who, Agatha said, had willingly donated them). She had wrapped them up in clingfilm and sent them to the newsagent, who had barred her from his shop for nicking crisps a week previously. Aged six, she had set fire to twelve bungalows in Lower Rottington and changed her name by deed poll to "Lord Gangrene". It had taken a lot of effort (and extortionate administration fees) to have it changed back.

☆ ☆ ☆

After she had visited the villa, Margaret had sped to the police station and kindly informed them that they needed to find Agatha at once. How on earth had they missed the tag going off? Wasn't this the reason she *had* a tag in the first place – so she could be located after curfew? Margaret, who had saved a pickled onion in the side of her mouth "for later", was in such a froth that she accidentally spat it out at Chief Inspector Coddlé.

"Who waz ze last person to see 'er?" he asked, uninterestedly.

"Of course, it w*aaa*s me, Inspector, but it is more important to focus on her very best friend in Fr*aaa*nce, Demone Can*aaa*rd. I have spoken to her parents and they tell me that she has gone to Paaaris because she believes that A*aaa*gatha is there. She must be right, they were so close..." Margaret sniffed a bit. There was a job to be done and if she could find Agatha quicker by crying then she would be happy. *And*, if she could take the spotlight off herself – since it was she who had let Agatha out knowing she would not be back until after curfew — so much the better.

"Demone knew more about my beloved sister than *aaaa*nyone else in the whole world…" concluded Margaret. Then, checking herself: "Ap*aaa*rt from *moi*, clearly. Find both of them for me, officer. *Find them*."

If Margaret had learnt anything, it was that Demone was never far away from a computer screen. Hadn't Agatha mentioned it at the flat? And surely, if Canard was near a PC, then the police would be able to track her down easily. In addition, if Demone *also* managed to find Agatha, then — hurray! — she would have done everyone's job for them.

In this modern world, there is no hiding place. In this briiiiiiiiiiiiiiiiiiiiiiiilllllllllllllllllllllliiiiiiiiiiiiiiiiii-iannnnnnnnnnnnntttttttttttt techno-landscape of CCTV and satellite tracking, you are never invisible for long.

Right enough, when Demone had got off the train in Paris, she had walked straight into the nearest cyber café. The police located her within minutes.

15. LE DEJEUNER SUR L'HERBE
INTERNET CAFÉ

Demone was relieved to be in front of a computer again. The journey from Brioche had been long and her fingertips had been itching to get back on the keyboard. She ordered an extra large *pamplemousse frappé* from *le garçon* and some snails in garlic sauce. Then she heard a sound. Her small spiteful face creased up like a thin plastic bag in a microwave. Her eyelid flickered and she twitched. It seemed that someone was giggling at her. She looked around but saw nothing. She heard whispering: *it's the frogs' legs girl!* This was highly embarrassing; Agatha had made her a universal figure of fun.

Demone had sometimes confused her virtual life with the real world. The trouble was that in cyberspace —

within the confines of the computer screen – she had proved endlessly popular. She had 3,457 friends on Bebois.com, including the very famous Vanessa Porcupine and someone who had been in an insurance advert. But in reality things weren't so clear-cut – and now the worlds were colliding. In the last few days her social network had unravelled – and all because of Agatha's footage. Demone was all too aware that her computer profile now accurately reflected real life: she had no true friends at all.

Oh, poor Agatha! This time, Demone planned to wreak a revenge that was so bitter, so awful, so revengey – that Agatha would never be able to face the public again. Or something along those lines.

"Terabytes!"

Canard started plotting, scheming, planning and conspiring. She tapped frantically on the keyboard: surfing the web, logging on, verifying details, logging off. She became confident again, clicking here, clicking there. This would be her finest hour! The greatest trick played on that abomination from Rottington Town.

When she next accessed her webmail, her inbox displayed a new message:

To: Canard, Demone <demone.canard@bebois.com>

From: Gendarmes, The <police.france@policey-world.net>

Time: 09.12 CET

Subject: Le Law

Bonjour Mlle Canard. We are the police – you may 'ave 'eard of us. We 'ave – through the wonders of ze technology – noted zat you are sitting at zis computer and we 'ave alerted Margaret Bilke. She is getting off the plane, leaving 'er luggage at Ze Ritz 'otel, then coming to you. She zinks you know where 'er sister iz and so do we. She will be zere soon.

Yours forcefully!

The Police (French division).

(If you would like to unsubscribe from these emails: you can't. We are the Law and you can do ze little to stop us.)

So, Margaret Bilke is coming! How can I involve her in my plan? thought dastardly Demone. She didn't want Agatha's sister to ruin the big showdown. If she befriended the woman, pretended to like the things she liked, she might get invited to her hotel. Now that was a fine location for Demone's grand finale! She was just about to hit the "delete" button when she heard some singing: *"Achetez le Burp Burp! / Avez vous le slurp slurp?"* Demone's face tightened. She turned around.

Demone planned to wreak a revenge that was so bitter, so awful, so revengey...

"Zut alors! C'est Agatha Bilke!"

Agatha had raced from Holbeck's lawyers to the nearest café for a sit down and a think. And whose mean little dark head had she spotted at the desk in the corner? Her old "chum", Demone! She had been surprised at first, but now she just wanted to see her squirm. She sang the song again, and added:

"How are your friends on Bebois?"

Demone's tiny cheeks flushed. Of course, they had all disowned her. But why was she taking this stick from the English oddball? Didn't she have other things to do? Like starting a chain of events that would rip through the rooms of the Ritz like an antelope with heartburn? Agatha would soon wish she had never been born! *Ahahahahahhahhah!*

At the great cathedral of Notre Dame, rebuilt in the twelfth century, gargoyles on the roof gaze down at the visitors below. They look like bad-tempered goblins; watching the whole of Paris as it goes about its daily affairs. Do they frighten people away from the city? Or maybe welcome them in? Demone was like a gargoyle, set atop cyberspace, watching out for the comings and goings of people she didn't like. And now Agatha was standing before her. She had rarely experienced an evil thrill like it.

"Garçon! More snails please! *Ahahahahahah!"*

Margaret, who had been informed by the gendarmes of Canard's location when she got off the plane at Paris, now entered the café in a flurry of flouncy shoulder-pads and strong perfume. She was delighted to see that the French girl had already found her sibling. How exciting – what a talented young computer fan!

"*AAAAAAAAAAAAAAaaaaaaaaaaa*gath*aaa*?" The vowels rumbled at them like an old rollercoaster on a windy day. "You've been found!" She approached her sister and gave her a big kiss on the forehead. Agatha winced.

"Snails all round!" cried Margaret, who thought that finding her little sister heralded a new and entirely profitable period in her life. She could not have been further from the truth. The spaghetti in her mind was getting mushy again.

It was only when Agatha started to hit Demone repeatedly in the mouth "by accident" and the French girl hit back harder that Margaret had to face up to the reality of the situation. The two girls could not bear each other.

16. THE CATACOMBS

The security guards led Holbeck out of the offices of Snippez and Snippé. It was lunchtime now and the boy was hungry. He snivelled as he was told he was headed for Les Catacombs Centre Pour La Détention Des Garçons Horribles (or the CCPLDDGH for, um, short).

This was no ordinary correctional facility and a far cry from the idyllic villa in Cannes. There was little fun or cake-making to be had – and you would not have been able to find it on the map. It was buried deep in Paris's secret underground tunnel system. Funded by the government, it was one of those places that was quite dreadful, but cost a fortune. (Like those special centres for famous people who like staying out all night and have to be told to stop by professionals.)

Originally limestone quarries from the Roman era, the Parisian catacombs had been converted into a mass tomb near the end of the eighteenth century. Thousands upon thousands of skeletons lay there, sitting neatly in rows as if they were table legs stacked in a cheap furniture show-room. Skulls decorated the mounds, as tidily arranged as the *femur* and *humerus* bones.

The catacombs were accessed by manholes in the street or ancient doorways that only the locals knew of. There were still some trap-doors, although most of these had been covered for years. They led straight to the horrors below, unbeknownst to tourists and the like. The people who had heard of the catacombs spread wild myths about them. One tunnel was said to lead to a sealed room which was full of flies. If by any chance the whole of Paris sneezed at the same time (according to SillyPedia.com, this was said to have happened in Ancient Rome with appalling results), then the network would erupt, spewing forth a pulsating mass of bluebottles. Another rumour claimed that the famous kidnapped racehorse Moulin Rouge was under there, and had started his own jazz club that was only open to a select few.

The CCPLDDGH was situated in a big crypt that held the bones of the cemetery of St Nicolas des Pommes,

placed there in 1804. The crypt was made up of a few dark rooms, which formed a sort of "knot", connected via miles of underground tunnels to other large crypts and tombs. Of course, being placed in any of the crypts was fraught with danger; the quarries could cave in at any moment, but the authorities did not seem to care. This was a sure-fire, quick-fix solution for all sorts of errant children. Instead of giving them therapy, a few days in this petrifying place saw a swift end to bad behaviour.

As Holbeck was escorted through the streets to a dirty manhole cover which led to the crypt, he was not optimistic. He was convinced that he would be banged up for ever because his parents had given up on him. He clutched Margaret Bilke's eviction letter in his hand. Yes, Agatha had tricked him... But then he had also wronged her. He should never have lied – whether he had thought she was Fifi or not.

☠ ☠ ☠

By the time Holbeck got underground, his old limp had come back and he was experiencing palpitations. It was deathly dark. The ceiling dripped water and he was alarmed that when he'd thought he'd seen *all* the bones in the world, there were more round the corner.

He'd had to walk a mile along a dank corridor with a big security guard. It twisted and turned until they were deep inside. Holbeck was petrified. Le Monsieur, who was meant to be brave and strong, started wheezing.

Skulls leered at him; cobwebs brushed against him; spiders and ants started crawling over his eyes and into his ears. A rat drew a picture of a tiny barge on his neck. The skeletons of several thousand rats descended on his head and his arms fell from their sockets. Of course, nothing like this happened at all, except in Holbeck's lively imagination. But it was all too much for the poor boy and he started jabbering.

"Let me out of here! The skulls of the skeletons and the ectoplasmic endomorphs! The spiders of the mind in the bathtub of the bewitched!"

"Do not worry," said a prison guard as they got to the entrance of the detention centre. "Ze leetle insects only come at night. Except, aha, we are in ze dark all the time so zey are here already!"

"*AAAAAAAAAAAAAARGGGGGGGGGGGGGggggghhhhhhhhhhhh*" screamed Holbeck, and fainted.

17. THE FURIOUS KITTENS

The furious kittens did not stay long in the Villa de Mer after Fifi and Le Monsieur left. They wandered around the place for exactly 23 minutes, not knowing what to do with themselves. They missed their leader and wanted to be with him. Cake-making was not the same; sitting in the treehouse seemed dull; even painting on the walls with fluorescent markers had lost its edge.

"There's only one thing for it!" cried a decisive Albert Citron. "We follow him up to the capital!"

It had taken them a long time to complete the journey. The twenty or so children had decided to get a boat – but it only took them around the harbour – after which they had become mixed up in a film premiere and signed autographs until their wrists ached. When they had got onto a coach bound for Paris, they seemed to have taken a route that involved first stopping off in Brussels.

Finally, they arrived. "We are *les chatons furieux!*" they sang as they wandered around the streets, holding a big banner with a picture of the whole group. It read: "Have you seen Le Monsieur?" They were convinced that Paris was a lot smaller than Cannes, and that everyone would have heard of their guru because he was always telling them that he exerted great influence in the city. They believed that wherever he was, their unfailing "Le Monsieur" radar could find him. If their leader was a needle in a haystack, they would have been able to sift through the straw and find that pin. He was theirs; they were born to all be together! *Chatons for ever!* Ra ra ra.

They were dismayed when this did not turn out to be the case: Le Monsieur was nowhere to be seen. The streets were filled with strangers; the cars roared past and there were a lot of lorries. The country bumpkins grew more and more despondent; they did not understand this grimy urban landscape. There was so much noise... and pollution; plus big buildings and men with very hairy bits sprouting up over their shirts. The kids were far away from fields and hammocks: the good life. Erk.

Dusk fell – like a hammer onto a trifle, so brutish they

"We are les chatons furieux!"
they sang as they wandered around the streets...

found the city – and the kittens were beginning to give up hope. It was here that one of their crew – a certain Albert Citron – had an accident. *Someone*, it seemed, had left a manhole cover open – a terrible thing to do! The tiny boy fell down the hole and yowled.

"Eeeeeeeeigh!"

He gripped onto the rim of the hole in the vain hope he could be pulled out. His little face was pale and scared – what was down there? If he fell, would he survive?

"I'll get you!" said brave little Chi-Du – but as he reached out Albert fell into Les Catacombs Centre Pour La Détention Des Garçons Horribles.

The other nineteen kids looked down the crater, trying not to topple over each other. They could all hear a faintly familiar sound.

"Shhh!" said one. "It's Le Monsieur! It sounds as if he is crying!"

"We must save him!" shouted nine-year-old Pliny Bovary. They abandoned the banner and scrambled down the manhole, one by one. As they heard his wailing they had a renewed sense of purpose, buoyed by their discovery. Even as they confronted the old bones of long-dead locals, they were happy. *Les chatons* were a formidable team.

"We are *les chatons furious / And we are very curious!*"

☆ ☆ ☆

The kittens' parents got to Paris just as their offspring were slipping down into the drains. They had no idea where to start looking for their children. The grown-ups had hand-written some flyers on the way up, which they duly distributed to passers-by. Agnes Bovary smiled faintly as she gave out those precious strips of paper – but the Parisians hardly looked at them before tossing them to the ground. It was so disheartening. She stared back at the crowds – why were they so uninterested? Did they see this sort of thing every day? Someone took a handful of flyers, thinking they were a discount for gym membership or buttons, then threw them all on the floor. Agnes stooped to retrieve the discarded slips and, as she did so, she made a breakthrough.

Madame Bovary saw that she had got an old rag stuck to the bottom of her shoe. Grimacing, she pulled it off and then looked more closely – it was some sort of banner with pictures of children... *their* children! This was a vital clue.

"Our darlings must be nearby if they dropped ze banner here!" she shouted to Rudolphe Citron, who was now looking tired and wan (he had a lot to cope with as a single father).

"They will have stuck together and are bound to be in a large pack – therefore *someone* should 'ave seen them. We are on ze right track!"

Citron was reanimated. He ordered everyone to keep their eyes out for any more evidence, then started thinking:

"Hey, when we woz talking to our children, what would zey think of when we discussed Pareeee?"

"The Eiffel Tower, of course!" said Madame Bovary, eyes flashing like disco bells. "We must go to ze tourist attraction, now! Our leettle angels will be cold!"

"It's the best idea anyone's ever had!" whooped Rudolphe. "Zey will certainly be there!"

The parents picked up their bags and hurried to the famous construction. They were headed in completely the wrong direction. They did not know that their "leettle angels" were under the ground instead of teetering over it, but they would not be told any different.

18. DROPLETS OF GREASY WATER

It was war in Le Dejeuner Sur L'Herbe. The fighting had reached stupendous proportions. Agatha had Demone by the ankles and Margaret was trying to grapple with a waiter's knee (entirely by mistake – she had been aiming for Agatha's shoulders). There were snails everywhere.

As someone who should be setting an example, Margaret Bilke really should, of course, have held back from joining in the fighting. It was her duty to guide her sister, not encourage her vicious streak. Soon, however, she realised that the two girls would just go on scrapping with each other for ever, holding onto each other's limbs like two octopuses at a karate club, if someone didn't stop them quick.

Margaret grabbed both heads and pulled them apart.

"*Wooooooooooooooaaaaaaaaaaaaaaaaaargh!*" she hollered, quite loudly.

"But this girl washed my clothes in dog food!" said Agatha.

"Zis girl put ze frogs' legs in ze toaster!"

"Said I was snotty on the internet and stole my passport!"

"She filmed it all!"

"*She* got me tagged!"

"Erm..." There was quiet at last. Margaret looked

The fighting had reached stupendous proportions

embarrassed; Demone looked triumphant.

"Zis was not *meeeeeeeeeeeee!*" she squealed. "It waz your sister who gave you up to ze police!"

Agatha glared at Margaret. She stared. She scowled. So it was her own flesh and blood that had betrayed her! She did not stop to think that this might have been for her own good – an attempt to monitor her every move so she did not get into trouble. She immediately went into a gigantic sulk.

"You *cannot* control me," she said. "I'm not going to do anything for you, from now on. I don't want to be near you. I don't want to hear you."

Agatha would have liked to have run away at this point, or start a nice big blazing fire, but there was very little that she could do right then. She may have been lied to by both Margaret and Holbeck, but she was in a foreign town with nowhere to go. She did not want to run away only to end up with some nutter in a *boulangerie*. So she just sat and looked grumpy, while the turncoat Demone chatted amiably with Margaret. The cheek!

"I do so love the sa*aaa*mba!" said Margaret, who was really feeling comfortable with this interesting young girl. They both seemed to share the same interests: dancing, pickled onions… Demone was good at putting Margaret at her ease and soon they were swapping numbers. Canard promised to come round to Margaret's suite at the Ritz later that afternoon, so they could chat further about dancing and share some pickled snacks.

As this grand friendship was being cemented, Agatha sat on the next table and did nothing. She was tempted to throw the old snail shells at Demone but she was both exhausted and fed up. The last few days had been a whirlwind – finding Holbeck and then realising what a twit he was. Staying with her sister then joining the Villa de Mer gang – but Margaret had reared her ugly head again. Agatha couldn't escape her. It wouldn't have surprised her if someone had handed her a new tag to put on her ankle. She was trapped.

Getting up from her table, Margaret started demonstrating some of her best moves. She gyrated and spun in front of Canard, tapping her feet as if she had crocodiles for toes.

"Wooh!" she huffed, and from her forehead sprang droplets of greasy water. As she pummelled the ground beneath her, Agatha felt her chair wobble. The more Margaret danced, the more the floor creaked, and before she knew it, the floorboards were buckling and loosening beneath her.

And then she was falling...

"*Arghhhhhhhhh nooooooooooooo!*"

Agatha tumbled through darkness – bump, thonk... then found herself ~~splat!~~ on a filthy concrete floor. She appeared to be in some underground tunnel. All she saw was dust and ~~currant buns~~ a pile of skeletons. She could hear Margaret caterwauling from above, and dimly made out her older sister's poppy eyes staring down into the abyss: "A*aaagaaaaa*th*aaaa*?"

The café manager rushed up.

"Please! Do not sue!" he exclaimed. "Zis is most unfortunate. There was once a hole 'ere, you see, an entrance down to ze catacombs. You have heard of ze catacombs, I presume? Don't worry, please... Your zister iz in safe 'ands. She 'as actually landed in a detention centre filled with officials etc. Where you are based?"

Margaret proudly shouted that she was staying in the Ritz Hotel.

"Aaah!" The manager pretended to be impressed. "If she zimply states to ze official zat she is residing with you, she will be escorted zere immediately."

Margaret breathed a sigh of relief. A detention centre! Well, at least that was one less thing to worry about. She hollered down the hole: "I'm in the RITZ! The *Fraaaaaaaaaaaanglaise Suite!!!!!!!!*" and left.

Presuming that it would take Agatha some time to find someone and persuade them that she had a sister in high places, Bilke senior decided she might as well pamper herself before Agatha reappeared. Just a spa pedicure and perhaps some waxing.

19. GLASSES

Oh, evil without end! Oh, life without let-up! Why do we go through hardship and stress and come out the other side looking "a bit run down" and not triumphant 'n' glowing? It's certainly not like the movies, is it?

This was vaguely along the lines of what Holbeck was thinking, sitting in his "room" in the CCPLDDGH.

He penned a poem in his journal:

"A rat as big as a dressing gown,
Mould on the wall, the size of a coastal town.
Cellars full of posh boys with mumps,
Who haven't seen daylight for months.
Big, jangly bunches of keys that sit on the belts of hoary old
officials who confiscate your shoelaces in case you go funny in

the head and decide to end it all."

It was quite good, he thought. Perhaps all this "hardship and stress" had its plus points – boundless creativity – after all.

NB: no one had mumps but it was the only thing he could think of which rhymed with "months". "Moths" sort of worked, but he wasn't sure about that either. "Humps" would have been nice if there had been any camels in there. But there weren't. ~~Ughmlh.~~

Holbeck shared his dingy cell with thirteen-year-old Louis Etoile, who sat in the corner listening to his mp3 player. This behaviour was nothing Holbeck had not seen before, but the boy was unusual in the way that he dressed. Louis wore tiny pince-nez glasses, a huge powdered wig and purple tights. He was the son of an aristocrat – someone who obviously thought that if he dressed the child like a king he would receive better treatment. But the lad was unhappy. All he did was wait for a telephone call from his parents – which never came.

Holbeck wondered how his life had led him to this terrible conclusion – to be locked up for ever with a morose boy who was even posher than he was, never to see his friends or loved ones again. Should he write another poem about it?

Instead he re-read the eviction notice. It pained him to think that all that time Agatha had kept up the pretence of being Fifi le Feu when she could have told him who she really was. Agatha – *Bilky* – had betrayed him. He was quietly fuming and regretted ever inviting her to Paris. How short-sighted he had been! Why had he not remembered to put his glasses on?

But hadn't Agatha stormed out of the lawyers' accusing *him* of being vile and selfish? Yes, Holbeck had wanted money, but only to help build the children's future happiness. He was *not* a selfish boy – everything was for his furious kittens, his cause. And yet, if he was honest, he had wanted to escape the villa, to escape the group. He was finding the children's adulation hard to deal with. They expected so much of him – Holbeck Folbeck – just an ordinary boy from Peerage Avenue, Rottington.

Perhaps he *was* only in it for himself, and Agatha had been right to try and evict him.

Thump thump, clonkety clonk!

He heard the drums from Louis's headphones; how much that boy loved his tunes. If only Master Folbeck, the heir of a dwindling fortune, could feel passion for something and not just bask in the comfortable cynicism he had thought was his birthright. He had pretended to love Fifi, hadn't he? What a callous thing to do! Where was his *soul*? And when he was at the villa, hadn't he been embarrassed by the kids' sheer enthusiasm? It was *they* who believed the dream, *they* who had created the perfect childhood – not he. Holbeck just wanted the power and cash. He wanted to stay in Cannes with his feet up and not letting anyone watch the telly. He was disgusted with himself.

His past showed a similar disrespect for ~~mothers~~ others. At boarding school, Holbeck had sold boxes of his parents' mints for a profit and made all the teachers cry. He had stolen the other boys' clothes and they had had to buy them back from him. He had upset the deputy head's cat by telling it about how the regime in the Far East treated domestic pets. He (Holbeck, not the cat) had been expelled from one school, then the next... and so on.

And now here he was... a cry baby. He had not really stopped blubbing since the moment he got to the catacombs, although it was now a low-octane sniffle. He paused for a moment – and heard voices.

"Le Monsieur! Where are you?" came the call. *Oh my word!* thought Holbeck. Could it be that the kittens had somehow found him?

"*Nous sommes les chatons furieux! / And we will save vous!*"

It *was* the children!

Their miserable leader did not know what to do. How could he continue as their guru now he had been locked up? He looked terrible, he felt terrible. His foot hurt and his head swam. He was useless: a washed-up despot. Poor little tykes. He heard them getting closer and waited for the screams – surely the crumbling piles of bones would frighten them all to death? No, they seemed to be coping all right.

"What's zat noise?" Louis tore his headphones off, excitedly – as he did every half an hour or so. "Will I be released today? It 'az been three months!" He trembled and bit his bottom lip.

"It is only a troupe of my most ardent followers," moaned Holbeckm, "trying to se~ me free... but what is freedom?"

He was interrupted from his adolescent ~~rubbish~~ reverie by the voice of Pliny Bovary, addressing the guard on reception.

"Excuse me," she said. "We have come a long way and we need to speak to our mentor *now*. He is a posh boy, average height, wig... wears glasses. We are lost without him."

The guard looked bewildered and came and got Louis – who was posh and sometimes wore pince-nez. (Pliny had neglected to mention that Holbeck was English – and they were not to know he had recently thrown his wig to the ground and stamped on it.)

"Zis iz your leader? Prisoner 5344681? Hahahahahah!" the officer laughed loudly. "Louis can lead you, if you like… to your cell!"

Now the *children* were terrified. Who was this little creature? And where was Le Monsieur? They had heard him, just now, hadn't they, sounding a little sad…? They did not know that the guard was just teasing them.

As their teeth started wobbling and their knees chattering, there was a tremor that would have registered a billiony-billion on the Richter Scale. Everyone was scared stiff. Was this the End? The moment when the world caved in and there would be lots of wind, snow and some aliens? (Hadn't Le Monsieur mentioned this a few weeks ago, when everyone was misbehaving?)

Crrrrrrrrrruuuunnnnnch! came the sound.

Crrrrrrrrrruuuunnnnnch! again.

This was not in fact the apocalypse, but Agatha Bilke crashing through the ceiling, fresh from the internet café up above, and landing in reception next to the kids.

"Hey! It's the angry kittens!" said Agatha, surprised to see them. She glanced at her surroundings and suddenly felt quite chirpy. "Thank goodness I've escaped my sister and that nerd Demone."

This was not in fact the apocalypse,
but Agatha Bilke crashing through the ceiling

20. DOCUMENTS DE FREEDOM

"Fifi!" cried the *chatons* in unison.

"Kittens! Why are *you* here?"

Hearing her voice, Holbeck ran up to his cell door. He had been cowering from his followers, but once he knew it was Agatha he had to make himself known.

"*Bilky!*" he called through the grim old bars.

"Guards, let me out!" he continued. "I have to apologise to this fine girl now!"

Of course, he was under strict instructions not to be released. Only a formal letter from his parents or loads of cash would do it – and he had neither.

Agatha could hear her old acquaintance shouting in some far-off corner.

"I have nothing to say to you!" she yelled. "You have lied

to me – and to the children. You are a stuck-up *espèce d'idiot*."

"How can you talk to Le Monsieur like that?" said little Chi-Du. "He is kind and good. He teaches us to use our imagination, to play in the fields – to do everything my parents tell me not to. What is wrong with that? He is an exceptional mentor!"

All the children cheered and then started to chant: *"Free Le Monsieur! Free Le Monsieur!"*

Agatha decided it was time to tell the children who their mentor really was: Holbeck Folbeck, a well-educated boy from the suburbs.

"He has conned you all into thinking he is 'Le Monsieur'. He's just a bored rich kid!" she screeched.

The children didn't believe her, and started chanting again.

The officers had had enough. *"Back onto ze streets you go!"*

They seized the whimpering kittens by their collars, and chucked them out by the official Main Entrance (which was a little smarter than the manhole they had all fallen through). The young cats protested but the guards were stocky and strong.

"You are ze boy's sister, right?" A guard led Agatha to the Listening Crypt, where ~~convicts~~ boys were allowed to take family visits. "You found uz through the ceiling entrance, which is not very conventional but you are welcome anyway."

The boy's sister? Well, Agatha supposed, she did look very upper class in her fashionable clothes – perhaps it was best to let the guards think they were siblings.

The Listening Crypt was surrounded by *yet more* bones, stacked so straight they almost resembled wallpaper, and a couple of wooden chairs. Agatha imagined all the skeletons in the world – and wondered when they would outnumber living people. It was quite a grim thought. They both sat down; a guard stood at the entrance, guarding.

"Is this a prison?" Agatha sneered at the boy. "Did you break the law? I hope so. You should be banged up for ever."

"Oh, Agatha!" said the minted, minty boy. "I didn't do anything! I was sent by Snippé and Snippez. My parents have had enough of me."

"But you never saw them."

"They'd had enough of me *even though* I never saw them."

Agatha's fury began to subside. The boy in front of her looked lost; defeated. He wasn't the *grand fromage*; a cruel dictator. He was suffering. Alone.

"I think I've started some sort of cult, Bilky," he said, voice lowered. "I'm in deep. These children adore me. I ran away — *we* ran away — because I didn't think I could take the adulation. And, yes, we needed to... er... deal with the problem with the rent. But these children, they took it all too much to heart. Yes, I presented them with an ideal place to live, but I didn't think I would create a lost Eden; it was an accident. I had to get away, and I didn't want to go back to Mummy — or boarding school. And now I'm stuck in here and I'm afraid I owe your sister a lot of money."

Holbeck waved the eviction notice in front of her face.

Agatha hadn't noticed it had gone! Oh, what a terrible mistake. Now he knew that she was deceitful and mean too... that she had pretended to be Fifi le Feu and he had believed her.

But, contrary to what Agatha expected, he remained calm, apologetic even. The letter had eventually made him reflect on what trouble he had caused — not the other way round.

"I have wronged you and I'm sorry."

Agatha had an idea.

"You can escape! It's easy!"

"What? I'm stuck here until I get a letter explainin—"

"Listen, posh boy. That document — it's a *notice to quit*! If we give it to these guards then it will look like I have just handed you *notice to quit the catacombs*! Simple."

Suddenly Agatha recalled she had seen the child in the
wig and tights carrying round his music player

"But doesn't it have the address of the villa on it?" Holbeck scanned the text.

"Only on page two," said Agatha. "Just stuff that back in your pocket."

They both smiled, long and wide like two canoes.

Holbeck motioned to the prison officer that they were finished, and explained in French that his "sister" had the right papers to see him released. The man peered at the letter. It was clear he did not know much English as he read it over and over. A sum was printed on the first sheet: six months' rent. It ran into thousands. The man read it out loud and held out his hand.

"*Erm? Merci???*" Holbeck was unsure what they had to do, so he said thank you.

"*Le bail,*" announced the official. "*L'argent. La monnaie. Le dosh. 345,089 euros, s'il vous plaît.*"

"But we haven't got that sort of cash."

Master Folbeck had a couple of coins but that was all. "I am destined to this life of old limbs and stale baguettes!" he wimpered, girlishly.

Then Agatha remembered: the mp3 cover she had stolen from the Poulet Vuittonne boutique. That was worth a lot of money — but what use was it down here? Suddenly she recalled she had seen the child in the wig and tights carrying round his music player. It was *just* what he needed – a shiny new cover to keep the gadget in pristine condition.

Once Louis (banged up again in his cell) saw the luxury item, he almost fainted – it was a limited edition and he'd heard that all that celebs had one. Master Etoile retrieved his money (half a year's allowance), which had been stuffed inside his socks. He was *seriously* rich. He hastily gave the loot to Holbeck, who passed it over to the guard, who counted it very slowly and gave them a few euros back in change.

Agatha was victorious – she and Holbeck were free.

"But no more 'Fifi', please," she told him as they ascended a small stone staircase that would take them to daylight and the streets above.

"And no more Le Monsieur, *by jingle!*" Was it true that in this unkind and not-very-relaxing world of ours, filled with unruly children and sad boys wearing wigs, these two people were the happiest alive?

"Let's go and find my followers!" said Holbeck, confident they would still be waiting for him outside the Main Entrance. "I've made up my mind; I will tell the kids to go back home to their mummies and daddies."

21. A WEALTHY, HEALTHY FAÇADE

M argaret contemplated her circumstances as her corns
were filed, her toenails buffed and a bright pink
glaze painted over them. She was running away from all her
problems (although not literally; she was in a spongy chair-
type thing). The spaghetti factory in her mind was doing
overtime – a big splodge was forming, thick and fast.

Bilke senior was in the Ritz Hotel spa and while she was
pleased *not* to be relying on her silly sister for company, she
was annoyed. Agatha had, predictably, abandoned her when
she should have been dealing with the villa. She had fled to
Paris, and had now fallen down a hole.

Let her show up when she feels like it! thought the older
Bilke. *I will help her no longer!* Thank goodness Margaret had
befriended that lovely Demone and invited her over. They

would have some orange juice and pickled onion sandwiches, then go through a few of their favourite dance moves. It would be delightful.

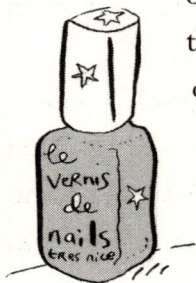

Still, Margaret knew that this was a distraction from the hard truth: she was stony broke. Not receiving the rent from the villa for so long – how would she pay for the suite, her toenails, even the train fare back to Rottington? She was on the brink of bankruptcy. How could she maintain the façade of a wealthy businesswoman? She started to break down – and so pretended she was having an allergic reaction to the nail varnish. (It was a way to get the pedicure free, at any rate.)

But Margaret was no ~~duck-billed platypus~~ quitter, no way. Margaret must attract wealth and turn it into, er, more wealth. She must think about money: touching it, smelling it, loving it. Wasn't that what all the articles in magazines suggested? *Positive thought. Ultimate suggestion. Get-me-some-cash-now-you-losers.*

She mused: maybe she could join the *Folies Bergères* and dance for a living. The renowned cabaret where ladies had performed saucy routines for over 130 years was still doing business. The girls were treated well and probably earned a fair bit. It didn't sound too bad, until she remembered that her not-so-nifty footwork had caused people to fall through holes into underground tunnel systems.

No, she could *not* get a job as a dancer. She was a money-maker, wasn't she? A seven-tiered cake of a woman. If *she* could not find hard cash with her stringy brains, then no one could. She would hatch a plan before her last nail was blow-dried.

The failed property owner peeked at the other people in the busy beauty salon. Funny, even a few men were having their eyebrows waxed and their hands crimped. Then she had an idea; perhaps not one that was entirely in keeping with women's rights, but one that might just get her out of a sticky situation.

Maybe Margaret could join the Folies Bergères and dance for a living

22. SURPRISE

The *chatons* were standing outside the entrance as Holbeck had predicted. They were shivering slightly, but instantly overcome with joy to see their leader. They tried to pick him up and carry him somewhere – but were foiled by the fact that a) their strength had been sapped by hunger and b) they didn't know where to take him.

"Look, guys," said Holbeck, mildly embarrassed. "You look like you need some grub. Bilky, do we have any change from the money Louis gave us?"

Agatha searched in her jacket pocket. She found a few euros and handed them to Albert Citron.

"Go and get some chips. Then, how do you fancy some sightseeing while we're here, what-ho? Myself and Fifi – I mean, Agatha, will see you at the top of the Eiffel Tower, *eh?*"

This was where Holbeck planned his big speech. No more *chatons*, no more summer camp. The children were going back home. They would look out over the majestic city of Paris and know that he was right. They could all keep in touch by email if they had to.

The kids ran off to the nearest bistro and soon Holbeck and Agatha became giddy with a sense of freedom and excitement. Paris was wonderful – they could get lost in it together!

They walked to the Eiffel Tower, laughing all the way. Up at the highest level, it really was a long way down. As Holbeck walked around the platform, the wind ruffled his hair, which made him look quite dashing. They could see the whole city, lurking like a favourite auntie below (and aunties do lurk, believe you me). Agatha was thrilled. If only they could camp out there and never go back down.

"Paris is ours!" shouted Holbeck. "Let's make it our home, eh, Bilky? I could write poetry and you could become a painter."

They walked around again. They did not have a care in the world.

"*Garçon!*" shouted Holbeck. "A magnum of your finest champagne!"

Of course, they did not have any wine on this level and

Holbeck was absolutely and utterly too young to drink, but it was funny anyway.

"*Mon dieu!*" a voice came from behind. And then: "*Le Monsieur!*" Holbeck turned around to see a group of out-of-breath parents running up the vast metal steps. They all started to shout at him.

HOLBECK
← AGATHA

"We 'ave found out about you and ze evil sect!" panted Citron, whose cheeks were so red they were almost green. "Give uz back ze children."

Instead of being afraid, Holbeck was pleased to see the fuming grown-ups.

"Certainly… when they get here."

"No, I zaid give zem back! I 'ave a book, *Culty Cults;* it details the 'orrors of nuts like ze *Le Monsieur!* Our kids 'ave been lovebombed into zinking zat zey are in ze grass zat is greener!"

"I said *certainly,*" repeated Holbeck. "They will arrive any minute."

Citron was confused; he had expected more opposition. Bovary nudged the irate father. "Ze boy doesn't seem like he is giving much of a fight, Rudolphe."

Agatha could hear chanting growing closer and closer – it was the children!

"Monsieur! Your chips!" Pliny Bovary had a big bowl of *pommes frites* she had brought up from the bistro.

"Oh!"

She caught sight of her mother and immediately dropped the bowl. Holbeck looked at them, yearningly. He was now ravenous.

"Pliny! Come to Mummy!"

Madame Bovary held out her arms for a cuddle but the young girl sidled up to Holbeck instead. She looked scared.

"Have you come to take me away from Le Monsieur?" she asked. "I will not leave his side."

"Pliny dear, do as your mother tells you," said Holbeck. "I am finding all this a bit... erm, claustrophobic. I am not your leader any more. It's time for you to go back to your parents now... And by a stroke of luck they are here!"

He grinned at the adults and tried to shoo away the growing army of followers that were collecting around him.

"But *you* are the daddy now," said Albert, born and raised in France but now speaking with an impeccable English cut-glass accent.

"Hear hear!" cried little Chi-Du. "I do not want to go back to lounging around and playing computer games. I want to build a sail boat and float up the Seine!"

"*Moi aussi!*" said another.

The children clung to Holbeck as if they were barnacles and he was a large sea rock. But he was not a rock; he was more like a strawberry jelly. That is to say, he was wobbly and quite fallible.

"Cease, my kittens!" he pleaded. "Look, I can't teach you what you *really* need to learn – maths, geography, history.

"Give uz back ze children!"

Childhood is not all climbing trees and poking insects with sticks. I don't know much French and I don't even have the wig any more, if you'd notice. Added to the fact that I haven't got any money to sustain the project. A perfect childhood is expensive, you know. Living the rural dream requires money, *pots* of it.. and that's something I have just run out of."

"But we don't care!" said Albert. "We love you!"

Holbeck blushed. This was the word he did not want to

hear. He started stammering and looked at Agatha pathetically. He couldn't cope with the adulation. What had started out as a means to stay in the villa had escalated out of control.

"Come back, Albert! You can watch as much TV as you like!" the worried father implored his son.

"I will *not* leave!" said Albert.

All the youngsters felt the same; they had spent so much time apart from their families, they no longer had any desire to go back to such normality — school, computer games, TV...

"*Ecoutez et répétez*, Le Monsieur," Citron approached Holbeck with a shiny, knuckly fist. "Be a man about it. Tell the children to come back NOW. *PROPERLY*. They will listen to you."

Holbeck started to address his followers, waving his fists around too, because he thought that might help.

"But I've said it all! Just go!"

The children did not move.

There was only one thing for it, thought Agatha. If Holbeck could not deal with the situation and let the kids go, then she would.

"You heard what the old guy said." Agatha was in fine form. "You have to *go*. No more hammocks, no more boats, no more dominoes. Yeah, you had a jolly time and all that, but the villa has been repossessed now. Go back and start anew — take the memories of the summer camp and weave them into the mundane reality of your life back home. Your parents love you! Holbeck doesn't. He thinks you're a pain in the —"

Holbeck gave Agatha a light kick in the shins.

Albert glanced up at his enigmatic leader — perhaps he *had* rather missed his parents — he'd certainly missed his pet rat. He slowly walked over to his dad. As he did so, the rest of the children followed. A few held onto Holbeck's velour jacket for a while until they finally relented.

The cult leader stifled a tear as he said *au revoir*. They had had a wonderful time, for sure. Now he must escape everyone before they started to ask too many questions.

"We have scaled the heights of pure adventure," he frothed as he started to descend the tower, holding onto Agatha to steady him. "We have dived into the cool waters of utter freedom, but all things come to an end, *pip pip*. The idyll will remain in our hearts, will it not? A dappled meadow we can visit when we wish… to see old friends and wander aimlessly into our dreams…"

Agatha made sure he didn't trip on the steps — his leg was really playing up by then.

But the speech was much too good. The kids chased after him; they could not bear to see their chap go. They still didn't believe he was some public school toff from Britain. For them he was and would always be... *Le Monsieur*.

"Come back!" they shouted in unison, starting to run after him. "We will do whatever you say!"

Holbeck hobbled down step by step with trusty Agatha, but he was not fast enough – the kids were catching up. On the very last step, Holbeck's legs buckled and he fell to the ground – not a great distance, it must be noted. There was a strange crinkling sound of bone against paving stones. He rolled over.

"Aaargh! *Pickles and frizz!*" he exclaimed, quite understandably.

The children circled him.

"Alas! We have maimed our guru!" yelled a frightened Pliny.

Then they all froze. Perhaps it was the cool realisation that the end had come. They call it "crunch time"; it's a bit like eating a lemon sandwich. Bitter but almost quite nice. The parents picked them up slowly and gave them warm, we-missed-you, you-can-watch-loads-of-TV-now hugs.

"I wish you all the best," said Holbeck. "Bilky and I – we want you to be happy. Take what you can and – *learn*. Study hard; go to school. Then, you too, will grow up to be —"

Agatha put a stop to this cloying speech, which would only have set everyone off again. "He means thanks," she said, and did a sort of "be off with you" gesture with her hands.

Steadily, the parents and children left, arm in arm ~~in arm in arm~~. They would be happy returning to their old lives, wouldn't they?

"We must get you some medical attention," said Agatha, when she and Holbeck were alone.

"I can always rely on you, Bilky," puffed Holbeck, smiling up at his wondrous saviour.

"You are my rock."

🏳 🏳 🏳

Before going in search of a doctor, however, Holbeck insisted that they visit Margaret. This happened to be the last thing that Agatha wanted to do. Her sister had snitched on her to the authorities and now claimed the calculating Demone as a friend. Agatha was fed up with luxury and high-status living.

"Where is she?" demanded Holbeck. "I need to apologise to her."

"She's at the Ritz," replied Agatha, who was confident Holbeck was bluffing. "Look, you need medical attention. A hotel is not the place for someone who has just fallen off the Eiffel Tower."

"Tremendous!" the boy replied. "They'll surely have a chaise longue and the number of France's top physician. I want to make good: I have seen the light and I know I have been wrong, so wrong – I must start repenting now."

Agatha was doubtful. Whenever she had said sorry in the past, it seemed that she had received no reward – spiritual or otherwise – in fact no one ever believed her. But she was not going to argue. Holbeck had his reasons. ~~Yeah right.~~

She found a small trolley nearby, used for carting souvenirs to the top of the tower. Holbeck sat as she pushed him all the way to the Ritz.

23. VISITORS

The Suite Franglaise on the sixth floor was empty when Agatha and Holbeck arrived. Staff had been surprised to see a girl pushing a trolley into the reception area, but once she announced she was the property developer's sister, they were attentive. They knew that the guests – of guests – always used the hotel's facilities, adding a lot of extras onto the bill, so they were happy to make Agatha and her invalid friend feel at home. (They had presumed Margaret was loaded when they spotted her Poulet Vuittonne keyring.) Agatha had signed the register "M. Bilke".

"It's for Marion," she explained. She didn't want anyone to know that she was there. She had had plenty of trouble already on this trip.

Having had a quick snoop around the suite, Agatha realised she was hungry and ordered room service. Lobster thermidor (the most expensive dish on the menu); two caviar pizzas; a quart of goji berry, pine nut and pomegranate juice and twelve bowls of assorted "executive" nibbles. She rang back to make sure that everything was served on silverware. *Then* she rang back and claimed she'd changed her mind again: *solid gold* was more the ticket.

At least it made Holbeck smile. He was becoming terribly serious and rather pompous – going on about "mending his ways". Agatha hoped they wouldn't stay there too long – when he was out in the Paris streets he was a lot more entertaining. Although he did have a habit of falling over.

They had rung for a medic and now had to wait. Holbeck clutched his leg and looked a bit like Jesus. Again, he had an air of self-sacrifice about him.

There was a knock on the door.

Agatha was surprised to see a small man in a fez-style hat, satin dressing gown and slippers standing before them. "I'm afraid zat I will 'ave to squeeze 'er in." In his hand he held a long lead... which was attached at the other end to an Indian elephant.

"I'm sorry, I think you have the wrong room." Agatha was rather confused.

"Agatha Bilke, *n'est ce pas?* Suite Franglaise, Ritz Hotel?"

The address was correct, but how did anyone know that she was there? The room was under her sister's name – they had been careful to give the doctor the "Marion Bilke" moniker too.

"Ahem," said the small man, as he pushed the elephant through the door. He held out his hand for payment.

Neither child had any cash. What was going on?

There was another knock. This time it was three chimps on a long chain. Then a fairground "test your strength" machine arrived; an art nouveau wardrobe; three sets of crocodile teeth; a tractor; a pair of trampolines and a deflated bouncy castle.

Each visitor demanded that Agatha give them "ze money you owe!"

"But you put in your 'best offer'!" said a large man who was wearing flippers. "Your feedback is 100%!"

There was only one explanation. After a lot of thinking, notes written on pieces of paper, four sums and Holbeck trying to ring a premium astrology line, the posh boy worked it out. Someone had been bidding on eBuy, using Agatha's details. They'd bought all sorts of stuff under her name, but this was not the end to it, she realised, as she watched the elephant steal the last few slices of pizza.

Other people were arriving – *young* people – with bottles of drink. They were wearing party clothes: paper hats, sequinned tops. They smelt of cheap perfume.

Soon the place was heaving with kids drinking out of plastic cups, various animals eating anything they could find, men and women shouting about money and, in the middle, Agatha Bilke, bemused.

Did she hear the key in the lock over all that noise? Perhaps not, but she was all too aware of the moment that her sister entered the room.

"Agatha, is th*aaa*t you? Meet Ger*aaa*rd Langoustine, he's a bulti-drillion*aaaa*ire!"

And then:

"Ohhhhhhhhhhhhhhhhhhhh n*ooooooooooooooooooooooooooo*!"

*Soon the place was heaving with kids drinking out of
plastic cups and various animals eating anything they could find*

24. WAYNE HEMINGWAY

Gerard Langoustine was a fine figure of a man. He was rich, handsome, ~~quite old~~ mature, full of elegance and utterly charmed by Margaret Bilke. He had met her while he was having a manicure downstairs. He loved English women – and here was one of them, staying in this very hotel! She'd invited him up for a drink "where we will have some time to ourselves" and he was full of anticipation.

When Gerard – and Margaret – walked into the Suite Franglaise they had a great shock. There appeared to be a circus in the main drawing room. Teens were drinking and passing out in the bathroom. A wardrobe had fallen on a pizza delivery

motorbike and the horn was sounding – a chimp was also trying to steal the lampshades.

Gerard legged it before Bilke senior could offer him a *jus d'éléphant*.

"Oh *Aaaaa*gatha! Why do you always h*aaa*ve to ruin everything? My sugar daddy! He's gone!"

It was worse than the mess at the villa – and Demone was due any minute. What would her new chum think of this? Margaret wanted to give up.

Her self-pity was interrupted by a caustic cackle coming from outside the window. The party-goers stopped their chatter, the chimps stopped nicking stuff and everyone else turned to look.

A head appeared at the lower window pane; the pinchy features of Demone Canard were unmistakeable. And she was laughing. At all of them.

"Demone! What are you doing?"

This was not the sweet, samba-loving girl that Margaret had met at the café. She looked like a goblin, staring through the window – a nasty goblin.

Agatha realised at once it was Demone who had set the whole eBuy thing up. She had sat in front of the computer in Le Dejeuner Sur L'Herbe, bidding for the strangest items she could find on the internet auction site. Then she had used Agatha's BeBois.com web profile to invite a group of random strangers to "the party of the year" at the hotel. *Now* she was recording it all on the new digicam she had bought with the rest of her Banque de Mayonnaise money.

She rapped on the window, demanding that someone open it so she could speak. A deranged, guffawing party-goer did so and Demone called through.

Demone was recording it on the new digicam she had bought with the rest of the Banque de Mayonnaise money

"*Ha ha ha*, Agatha! Spam! I have got my rev*onge*! And now," she continued, "log on, for *moi*'s worst trick of all: I shall film your party, send it to your parents *and* the police! You will be grounded for ever! I am coming in!"

Demone tried to scramble in through the window without dropping the digicam. She was standing on a small ledge and it was hard to hoist her tiny self up. She clawed at the sill, desperate to hold both the gadget and the frame.

"Hurrffklurgh! I am *still* coming in!"

Agatha watched her as she struggled. She really was the most rotten person she'd ever met.

"Murgghleeuooo! I am *still* —"

Suddenly, Demone lost her footing and disappeared. Exactly *how* she had climbed all the way up to the fourth floor was a-bogglin' in itself. This grand building, once home to illustrious types such as Coco Flannelle, G. Scott Fitzgerald and Wayne Hemingway... and now she was hanging off it.

"*Aaaaaaaaaaaaaaaaaaaaaaaaaaaaaaaaaaaaaaaaaaaaaaaahhhhh-hhhhhhh!*" The scream got softer and softer until, with a light thud, it stopped.

Holbeck hobbled to the window and looked down.

"She's gone. Dead," he said, sombrely.

Agatha wanted to cheer, but it didn't seem right.

Demone had been alive, and now she wasn't. There was a strange feeling in her left side.

Then the room heard an almighty sound coming from below.

"*Aaaaaaaaaaaaaaaaaaaaaaaaaaaaaaaaaaaaaaaaaaaaaaaaaahhhhh-hhhhhhh!*"

This time it was not Demone, but Louis Etoile screaming. He had just witnessed a person fall onto the top of his lovely velvety carriage outside the Ritz Hotel. He stood on the pavement, thankful that he had just stepped out of the plush vehicle.

"Are you all right?" he asked the tiny figure.

Dazed, Demone lifted up her head and looked around.

"Where am I?" she asked.

She was not *quite* dead after all.

25. CHARIOTS (NOT) OF FIRE

Louis Etoile's comfortable carriage had saved Demone from certain death. Parked outside the famous hotel to let the family out, it had cushioned her fall. Pushing Holbeck out of the way (quite rudely), Agatha looked out of the window herself and spied Demone.

"She's alive, you numbskull!" she shouted at Holbeck — then ran downstairs.

The strange silhouette of a boy in purple tights, with a large powdered wig on top of his head, talking to an evil computer geek, was a joy Agatha was so glad Demone wasn't dead! She didn't know quite why, given the facts of the matter, but she just was. And to see their old friend from the catacombs!

"Louis!" she shouted.

"Fifi!" he replied and with his spindly legs he ran over and gave her a spindly hug. As Demone was slowly hoisted off the carriage roof by trained medical professionals, Louis explained to Agatha that he had just been released from the detention centre and was now reunited with his mother and father.

"I cheered up after you sold me zat sumptuous mp3 cover," he said, clearly thrilled. "And so cheap! Zen I called my parents to tell them my good news, and zey zaid zat zey would take me home! All thanks to you! We are just popping in 'ere for a cocktail at ze Wayne Hemingway bar."

Louis Etoile's comfortable carriage
had saved Demone from certain death

Quite obviously, on a practical level, Agatha Bilke had not actually done anything to secure Louis's release. However, he now connected her with good fortune. She wasn't going to protest.

Louis pointed to Demone and the carriage, bemused. "Do you know zat girl?" he asked.

Agatha thought for a moment. She had been upset to see the girl fall from the hotel window. It hadn't seemed right that her life should be so cruelly snatched from her at such a young age. Agatha – not known for her wealth of human feeling – was glad that she was all right. But Agatha Bilke was not Mother Theresa. She was Agatha Bilke.

Agatha looked Louis squarely in the eye: "That girl? No, I don't have a clue who she is."

"Come and meet my mama and papa!" said Louis, taking Agatha's arm. "Where's zat nice young man you helped rescue from *le* detention centre, *oui?* We must go and 'ave a drink! You know, we will do anyzing for you, my family! *Anyzing!* I tell you! You saved *moi!*"

And off they walked, into the hotel and towards the bar.

26. SOME KINDNESS, AT LAST

Eventually, Agatha invited her sister to meet the Etoiles in the Wayne Hemingway bar. She felt bad leaving her alone in the wrecked suite, now that the unwanted visitors had gone. Here, everyone was getting on splendidly, especially Holbeck and Louis.

Margaret was talking to Louis's father, and he had just offered her financial assistance. After the "Demone Incident", Margaret could not pretend she was rich or happy. Her life had been ruined – but only for a few minutes. Monsieur Etoile had come up with an enticing proposal.

"So this loan is for the period of one year?" Margaret Bilke went through the paperwork with Louis's dad, who wore the same style dress as his son.

"Ah yes, *Madame*." He was a warm-spirited man. He did not like to see people without two euros to rub together.

"Now we 'ave found ze tenants for your Cannes villa, you should 'ave no trouble wiv ze repayments. And at our 0% interest rate you will find no other offer to match it."

Margaret was ecstatic. She was in the black once more, and if everything went to plan, she could add another apart-

olive?

ze contract
de Rental
loan

*"Now we 'ave found ze tenants for your Cannes villa,
you should 'ave no trouble wiv ze repayments"*

ment to her portfolio at the end of the year.

"But you are going back to ze Rottington?"

"Yes, I think I've h*aaa*d all I can cope with here." She smiled, like a dove who's won a hairdressing championship – a mixture of happiness and exhaustion. "A*aaa*gatha proved me wrong about that girl Demone. I think I can do better by managing my properties from England."

Madame Etoile nodded and looked sympathetic. She too was so grateful that Agatha had brought a little light into her son's life, and enabled him to phone them. He had previously thought that they were too busy to care; an all-too-familiar case of crossed wires. Happens in all families, really it does.

"But what are zees two young English *enfants* going to do?"

It was a valid question. Agatha and Holbeck were the only children left at the Ritz now. Demone was in hospital, and would soon be talking to the police. The party-goers had gone home. The furious kittens were all probably sitting at home eating crisps and watching DVDs. Plainly, Margaret had had enough and would not look after Agatha any longer. Her sister did not want to go back to her parents and Holbeck felt the same about his.

"If you would like, we could do ze extended French

exchange for you. Just until you sort yourselves out."
Monsieur Etoile was very kind. Louis smiled too, even
though he now had his headphones on.

"We 'ave a modest place, just outside ze capital. It may
be a little not your style but we call it 'ome. Perhaps you
would be interested...?"

Agatha, Holbeck and Margaret were delighted. The
Folbecks were contacted, via their lawyers, and they con-
firmed that they were happy to let their son stay for a while.
It did not take long before all the details were finalised. A
new life in France. The one Agatha had hoped for all along.

27. "OUR 'UMBLE ABODE"

As they walked around the Orangery, gazing at the fountains in the distance, Holbeck and Agatha sighed. After all they had been through, things had actually worked out. Very important doctors were monitoring Holbeck's leg and he was starting to walk properly again. The Etoile family seemed like the nicest people you could meet. They were generous, considerate, polite and – oh yes – stinking rich. Thank goodness for eccentric millionaires! Their "'umble abode", as they called it, was perhaps not the largest wing of the palace of Versailles – but it was no hovel. The *salon de chevaux* was the most inspiring room Agatha had ever seen.

"It's a shame my sister is not here to experience this," Agatha *almost* said. In actual fact she was glad Margaret was

The "'umble abode" was perhaps not the largest wing of
the palace of Versailles – but it was no hovel

far away — whatever she did, that woman only seemed to add to everyone's problems.

"You know, Bilky, we will have to return to Rottington some day," said Holbeck, as they passed the grand canal and a hedge in the shape of an ice cream sundae. "But maybe by then we will have grown up a bit — our families too — and we won't argue with each other all the time. You won't even dream you ever used to start fires, or lock people up in a mortuary. *Eh what!*"

They stood and contemplated the still waters before them. Wasn't life like a canal? thought Agatha. Quite cold and watery, and man-made. No, it wasn't like a canal at all, but the water looked nice at this time of year. Perhaps that was it — and just that. Life wasn't like anything — it was just life. She was glad hers had been less eventful during the past few weeks.

"Do you ever wonder, Bilky, what it would have been like if you *had* had the perfect childhood?"

Agatha hadn't, but she didn't want to dwell on the fact, not now.

"Whatever has happened to us has made us who we are."

Holbeck was coming over all pompous again, thought Agatha.

"I tried to give a perfect childhood to my kittens...

but... perhaps I needn't have bothered. Maybe they *were* better off with their parents."

They heard footsteps – ah, one of Holbeck's doctors was rushing over. Perhaps he had an update on his ankles.

"A colleague of mine has called!" panted the excited practitioner. "We were talking about you both, and he brings great news from ze Rottington General! You are ze kid wiv no 'eart, am I correct?"

He directed his gaze at Agatha. Why on earth did this have to be brought up here? Bilke thought she had left all that behind. When she was at the Rottington they discovered she had no heart and it had been a cause of turmoil... but far away in France she had forgotten all about it. This was the worst moment for the doctor to arrive, surely, as she and Holbeck were now getting on really well. Agatha wanted to run away and hide in a hedge, but instead she nodded.

"I am zat – I mean, *that* girl," she said, slowly, expecting the worse.

"Zey say it's all ze nincompoop!" laughed the doctor. "You 'ave got a little speck of one! Zey found it on ze x-ray."

Holbeck turned around and beamed.

"I didn't want to mention anything, Bilky, but I did think you were weird for a while – and now I know you're not!"

He threw his cane in the air in jubilation and she had to go and pick it up for him.

"*Merveilleux!*" grinned Agatha, revealing teeth that had not been cleaned for a while. "Sorry I called you a numbskull at the Ritz, Holby."

"I will just 'ave to get a copy of ze photo sent over in ze next few days!" exclaimed the physician, and scurried back to the palace.

"Perhaps..." Holbeck was wistful. "We could stay here for ever..."

Again, they silently observed the calm waters before them. *Scratch scratch!*

There was rustling – if not yer actual scratching – from the hedges. A small head popped out amidst the box leaves.

Albert Citron.

"Le Monsieur!"

"I'm sorry, it's Holbeck now." The posh(ish) boy was stumped. This wasn't in the plan.

"Le Monsieur Holbeck! I have returned! I could not live without you!"

The child was shaking; he was overjoyed and overcome. He had spent time away from his leader and it had not been right.

"See, child... *mon petit chaton*, this is someone else's

house. I cannot be your leader, I'm done with all that now. You're free, do you hear? *Free*. Go back to Mummy and Daddy! Eat pizza!"

Albert looked downcast.

Just then, another rustling sound.

"Le Monsieur!"

This time it was Pliny Bovary. No sooner had she started to speak than another child appeared. Then another, and another. The furious kittens had come back to their beloved guru.

"Aw," said one, still aping the English accent. "You and Fifi look so good together…"

Bilky looked at the substantial property which dominated the horizon. Surely there was room for a few of the kids to go undetected for a while…

EPILOGUE

As Inspector Coddles' train pulled in at Paris Gare du Nord, he checked his notes. One Agatha Bilke, whose electronic tag had fallen off. He checked the time – good heavens! She had been missing for weeks now! How was it that he had only just been alerted to the fact? Didn't the French gendarmerie ever do their job properly? He was going to have to launch a full-scale enquiry in order to find her. It would not be easy.

☆ ☆ ☆

As she walked into the BureauStar Executive Departure Lounge, Margaret stopped to look at the Duty Free shop. She had missed her old acquaintance Coddles by minutes.

She espied the fine wines, expensive chocs, diamond jewellery and rows of perfume that decorated the shelves like lights on a Christmas tree. Had Margaret grown tired of luxury? Could she see through its gilt façade? It now reminded her of the past few days, which had been quite difficult, to say the least. Yup, she was fed up with fancy stuff.

But she was entitled to a sniff of a bespoke scent, surely? She lolloped over to the extravagant bottles and waved her ~~hooter~~ nose over one that was marked "*La Plume de ma tante*".

"Mmmm!"

Nearby was a small chair, used by the shop staff. Oh, how her feet needed a rest! Margaret was frazzled; she forgot herself as she bent over to light a scented candle that was on display. She wished to feel that deep sense of relaxation. Just a few *positive thoughts* before she caught the 19.55 to St Poncross.

"Mmmm."

The tannoy announced her train; the last boarding call. She must hurry.

With a swing of her jute shopper, an eco-friendly tote bag, she accidentally knocked over the candle. Soon the whole duty free department was in flames. The blaze travelled and within minutes much of the station was on fire.

Securely on the England-bound train, Margaret was pleased to be going home and that Agatha had found such sensible people to board with for a while. She liked the Etoiles – they were good, caring – and most importantly – *rich* people. She sighed and watched Paris glow in the night sky. So romantic...

This was all she noticed of the chaos left in her wake.

GLOSSARY

Breton jumper
A blue and white stripey top made famous by painters who liked pretending they were in the Navy when they wore them. Or something.

Escargots
Snails. Often to be found in garlic butter. (Or in a field... just about to be covered in garlic butter.)

Une fille très difficile
Agatha Bilke

Une fille très très difficile
Demone Canard

Garçon!
Waiter!

Garçon! Je voudrais des escargots, des pommes frites et des oignons marines, s'il vous plaît. Zut! Les gendarmes!
Waiter, I would like snails, chips and pickled onions, please. Oh no! The police!

Gendarme
A policeman of the French variety, usually has a moustache, lives in a gendarmerie. As for lady policemen, they are called *mademoiselles-gendarmerettes*. Probably.

Jus de cantaloupe
A nice melon-flavoured juice drink — nothing to do with elephants.

Oignon
Onion, actually. Not to be confused with a horse.

Le petit chien
A tiny dog. In France they make them
so small (FYI in a factory in Brioche) they
can fit into a Poulet Vuittonne card-holder.
Some of them can be worn as earrings.

Le Petit Dejeuner Sur L'Herbe Du Temps Perdu
A famous French book written by an old man.

Poulet Vuittonne
France's foremost luxury luggage label.
For this season's collection, bags made
from the hide of the 2007 Husky Sled
Team are scrawled on by famous artist
Richard Pricey, and sold for thousands
of euros to rich people who cannot read.

Savon
Soap. All nice soap comes from France. Fact. That's why people pay
over the odds for a block with bits of grass in it.

S'il vous plaît!
Please!

Zut!
An exclamation of surprise or horror, often goes with "*Alors!*" and "*It's
the mademoiselles-gendarmerettes!*"

ALSO BY SIÂN PATTENDEN

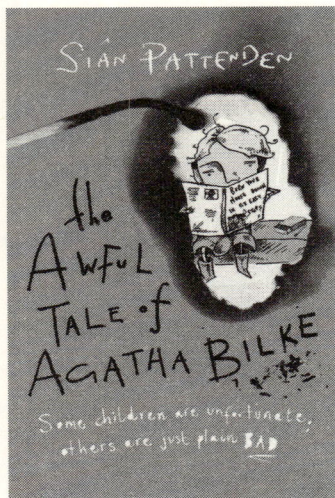

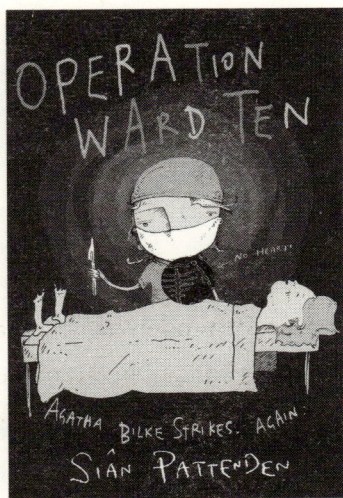

The Awful Tale of Agatha Bilke

Most girls are lovely. They smile and laugh and skip. They put fancy ribbons in their hair, they collect kittens, they sing about helping hungry people (even the greedy ones).

And then there's Agatha Bilke.

Agatha is mean and selfish and bent on causing harm. Her parents despair of her. They send her to the TreadQuietly Clinic for Interesting Children, a "therapeutic" boot camp for oddballs where she meets all sorts of other problem kids. However, none of them are prepared for Agatha – least of all the people in charge, the bumbling Humphrey doctors, who seem powerless to stop her in her bid for destruction.

£5.99 ISBN 978-1-904977-51-3

Operation Ward Ten

In this hilarious sequel to *The Awful Tale of Agatha Bilke*, Agatha performs routine heart surgery, carjacks an ambulance, runs her own sister over and uncovers the cause of a National Disaster. But what has she done with Cauliflower? And can she stop "Holby" finding out her terrible secret?

£5.99 ISBN 978-1-904977-89-6

Siân Pattenden has been a journalist for a few years, working for publications including *Smash Hits*, *NME*, *The Face* and the *Guardian*. She has also been on the telly and radio. She is married to songwriter Luke Haines and has a son called Fred. They live in London. Her first book, *The Awful Tale of Agatha Bilke,* published in 2006, was short-listed for the Glen Dimplex Award, the Sheffield Children's Book Award and the Branford Boase Award. Her second book, *Operation Ward Ten,* was published by Short Books in 2007.

For more on Agatha and her world, check out Sian's website: **http://sianpattenden.co.uk**